MAKING
MBO/R
WORK

MAKING
MBO/R
WORK

ARTHUR C. BECK, JR.
ELLIS D. HILLMAR

*Institute for Business and
Community Development
University of Richmond*

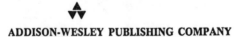

ADDISON-WESLEY PUBLISHING COMPANY

*Reading, Massachusetts
Menlo Park, California
London · Amsterdam
Don Mills, Ontario
Sydney*

ISBN 0-201-00469-0
FGHIJKLMN-DO-8987654321

FOREWORD

Few people argue with the logic of MBO. In fact, most major corporations and an increasing number of government agencies, especially at the federal level, purport to use Management by Objectives. Yet, the nagging question still remains: How do we make it work? Arthur Beck and Ellis Hillmar have devoted many years to uncovering the answer to that question and present their conclusions in this important book.

Two distinctive features about their approach have been identified with the authors. The first is that they aren't content to have people set goals and then forget them. Like Schleh and other systems experts, they insist that results must be factored into the MBO process. Otherwise a manager who wants to manage by objectives might think he has done the complete job when he sets goals. If this were true, then anybody could win an Olympic medal. All that would be necessary would be to define the distance and time: "Run 100 yards in eight seconds." The trouble with this is that many people simply couldn't do it, and they might be deluding themselves and others if they assumed that setting goals alone makes everything perfect. MBO calls for steady evaluation of results and feedback and correction.

The second major feature is that the authors are concerned about the group makeup, group processes, and team building before crunching everyone into an orgy of writing out goals. They come down clearly in favor of the OD-before-MBO approach rather than the reverse. This approach has been used with great success in many organizations.

McClelland's Achievement Motivational system suggests the adopting of goals, speaking the language of success, building systems to support success, and finally building group effort toward goals. The authors of this work don't disagree with that four-part approach, but suggest that the order should be reversed: build teams first.

I suspect that both approaches have worked, and you can learn something useful which may fit your organization when a more directive approach to goal setting from top-down has failed.

George S. Odiorne
Dean and Professor of Management
School of Business
University of Massachusetts, Amherst

PREFACE

While working with managers in many different systems—business, government, health care, education and religious—we have found the typical approach to Management by Objectives to be a highly mechanistic one. Managers have often said that they have had objectives for years and consequently have always managed by objectives. These experiences and interchanges have led us to write *Making MBO/R Work* to clarify our approach to the concept. We also want to help managers realize the implications of the concept while deciding whether MBO/R is right for their organization. It is very important for managers to be aware of the effects that MBO/R will have on them and their organizations.

The condition we hope to create—our goal in writing this book—is organization RESULTS managed through an effective goal setting process. Obviously, this book alone cannot accomplish that, but it can be *one* effective tool for making it happen.

BACKGROUND

We are members of a team of organization consultants at the University of Richmond's Institute for Business and Community Development. As a part of that development activity for the past nine years we have worked as consultants and trainers in Management by Objectives for RESULTS. Three years ago, *A Practical Approach to Organization Development through MBO—Selected Readings* was published. (We think that the basic readings in that book are still appropriate. It is a good text to use in conjunction with this book.) *Making MBO/R Work* is another step in our growth and development in applying this concept. It is a direct result of our integration of research and application experiences during the past three years. It is where the state of the art is for us now.

With the flow of good data in books and articles from many practitioners in the field, we expect our growth and development in MBO/R to continue in the years ahead. We have much to learn about the application of this dynamic concept which can be very different in different organizations. Managers in each organization need to be aware that the MBO/R system they use may be different from the system used in other organizations. The concept remains the same but the words, the methods, and the procedures will vary.

ORGANIZATION OF THE BOOK

Making MBO/R Work is organized into three parts. The first six chapters cover the managing aspects of the concept and the factors that influence the management climate, such as values, power, the individual, and RESULTS. This helps explain the relationships among the organization development, MBO/R, and open-system concepts. Chapters 7 through 15 cover a step-by-step model for implementing the MBO/R concept. This model can be used for diagnosis and as a basis for developing an MBO/R system in an organization. Skills and competencies for successful implementation are described in Chapter 16.

ACKNOWLEDGMENT

Our work at the University of Richmond has brought us into contact with many outstanding consultants in MBO/R and organization development. We have learned from these individuals with whom we have had personal contact, and from others through their writings. Most of all we have learned from our clients who have shared their work and their experiences with us and have tolerated us within their systems. Though we have had some failures, we have had many successes. Even with the so-called failures, we receive periodic feedback on increased effectiveness observed in individuals and groups within those organizations.

Specifically, we would like to acknowledge the help we have received from our colleague, Richard S. Underhill, who has stimulated our thinking with a holistic approach to the concept. Specific help has been received from Frank R. Hinton, and John C. Talbot. The writings of Dale D. McConkey, George R. Morrisey, George Odiorne and W. J. Reddin have had considerable influence in developing our approach to the MBO/R concept. We are indebted to Joyce Faison and Yvonne Ware for their patience and assistance while typing the various drafts of the manuscript.

Richmond, Virginia   A.C.B.
January 1976   E.D.H.

CONTENTS

1 The Management Aspects of MBO/R   1

2 Values and Their Effect on Individuals and Organizations   7

   Adapting to the New Work Ethic
   M. Scott Myers and Susan S. Myers   13

3 emPOWERment - Developing Personal Power to Support
   Authority Power   32

   The Development of Power Relationships in Management
   John C. Talbot   38

4 What Really Counts for Me?   57

5 What Do You Mean, I'm Not Getting RESULTS?   63

   Grabbing Profits by the Roots: A Case Study in Results
   Management *Edward C. Schleh*   68

   Demand Better Results—and Get Them *Robert H. Schaffer*   80

6 Putting It All Together for Organizational Effectiveness   93

   Emerging Perspective about Organization Planning and
   Development
   J. Jennings Partin   97

7   MBO/R Navigation and Operation Systems   116

8   Mission - What Are We All About?   121

9   Role: Outputs and Relationships   128

10 Focusing on Effectiveness   136

    Effective Management Job Descriptions
    W.J. Reddin   138

11 Planning Analysis—Looking Ahead   159

    Planning Analysis
    Frank R. Hinton   163

12 Objectives: Management's Working Tool   167

    Measurable Objectives for Staff Managers
    Dale D. McConkey   173

13 Standards of Performance—The Basis for Evaluation   184

14 Now Here's My Plan!—Planning and Managing the Action   187

    The Position and Function of Budgets in an MBO System
    Dale D. McConkey   191

15 Progress and Performance Reviews—Feedback for
    Managing Accountability   203

    A Systems Look at Performance Appraisal
    E. Allen Slusher   210

16 Developing MBO/R Skills and Competencies to Make It Happen   220

THE MANAGEMENT ASPECTS OF MBO/R

Making MBO/R (Management by Objectives for RESULTS) work in an organization requires a significantly different approach to implementation. Relatively few organizations have dealt with "traditional" MBO as a total management process. Even fewer have worked with it using a systems approach. Both of these are inherent in the way we go about making MBO/R work.

In many of those organizations which say they have MBO there seems to be a serious lack of conceptual knowledge relative to what it's all about. As with Theory X and Y[1], many people are inclined to use MBO to describe a form of managerial behavior. However, MBO is truly a *concept* which may be implemented with a variety of behavioral patterns. Carvalho has described MBO as the name attached to the idea that people should know what kinds and amounts of results they want to accomplish before they start working toward those results.[2] Starting from this concept and developing a management process to implement it leads to a wide variety of possibilities in practice. This approach is considerably different from those situations in which MBO is presented as just another managerial skill or technique.

MANAGEMENT BY OBJECTIVES FOR RESULTS (MBO/R)

As we developed a goal setting process for implementing our approach to the MBO concept—MBO/R—we found it helpful to clarify our ideas about the various aspects: Management,

RESULTS, and Objectives. We think that management is the most important aspect for we believe that MBO/R should become the basis for the total management process within an organization. The expectation is that this will be a more effective way to bring about organization RESULTS, the second aspect. Within the basic title, <u>Management</u> by Objectives for RESULTS, we view objectives as the third most important aspect. Objectives are the means, or tools, to facilitate managing for RESULTS.

Many organizations emphasize objectives without any specific concern for using them as the basis for management or producing organization RESULTS. In this case, objectives are usually set once a year and soon forgotten until the next annual exercise. An example of this was brought to light in a conversation with a manager in an organization that had been using MBO for four years. The manager remarked: "We play games with MBO here. I tested it last year by taking my previous year's objectives, changing the dates, having my secretary retype them and submitting them to my boss on schedule. I have yet to receive any comment on them. No one checks whether I meet the objectives or not." In this situation the objectives were obviously not used in the managing process. There was no MBO accountability. MBO was not causing anything different to happen. It was another paperwork exercise imposed on the organization above and beyond the normal work effort.

In those organizations where it is a process used for managing, the various functions of management are all carried out in such a way as to ensure that the objectives will lead to the desired RESULTS:

- In *planning*, this will mean developing the strategies, tactics, and action plans to ensure achieving the objectives and organization RESULTS.

- In *organizing*, structures will be worked out to support accomplishing functional performance through objectives rather than organizing around activities.

- In *motivating*, the direction will come from within as a commitment to achieve the agreed upon objectives rather than through external coercion.

- In *controlling*, there will be more self-directed action in response to accountability for performance on objectives and the rewards for achieving organization RESULTS.

Though most texts and articles put considerable emphasis on RESULTS in MBO, particularly as a selling point, few have been clear in describing what that means. In Chapter 5 we will go into greater depth on the matter; but when we use the term RESULTS, we are referring to performances or outputs which are directly related to the realization of the organization's mission and goals. RESULTS are the actual conditions that exist when goals and objectives have been achieved.

Goals are the broader, long-term achievements expected of the whole organization. As detailed in later chapters, objectives are statements of the *desired* outcomes of work efforts by individuals and groups in the organization. This is the essence of the concept of MBO/R in which the boss and subordinate(s) come together to agree in advance on those desired outcomes (RESULTS) and then manage their achievement.

MBO/R AND ORGANIZATION DEVELOPMENT

When an organization begins to focus on RESULTS as described above and switches its emphasis to developing organization goals and integrating the individual's needs, it is into Second Generation MBO.[3] This shift from an individual orientation to an organization RESULTS orientation creates considerable pressure for skills in Organization Development (OD). Now there are individual, work group, and intergroup concerns to be managed as part of the goal setting process. Thus MBO/R has moved into group process which requires basic behavioral skills typical of OD technology.

What's OD all about? Organization Development is a planned, managed, systemic process to change the culture, systems, and behavior of an organization in order to improve the organization's effectiveness in solving its problems and achieving its objectives.[4] Because of its nature and concerns, OD interventions might fall into any (or all) of the following types of activity:

Team building
Job design/enrichment
Goal setting
Problem solving
Work climate/environment
Decision making
Managing differences/conflict
Process consultation
Diagnosis and feedback
Organization/physical structure
Interpersonal skills
Values clarification
Transactional Analysis
Managing accountability
Helping relationships
Gestalt applications in organizations
Open system concepts
Psychological contracting

In an earlier article we took the position that it didn't make much difference where you started in implementing MBO/R or OD because you would soon need to have the other to be truly success ful.[5] The theory base for each of these efforts comes together and requires integration when we begin to work MBO/R with a group orientation.

An "open system" approach seems to be most helpful in this situation for it moves beyond merely having both concepts function ing as two techniques in the same organization or system. The open system approach involves the consideration of all trends and forces which affect an organization, be they external or internal. It recognizes that everything is interconnected and must be worked from the context of the output of the larger system.

A related concept of systems analysis is appropriate for im proving our management approach at this point through the idea "think systems." Applying this as we analyze, diagnose, plan, implement, and evaluate would force us to constantly test our data to validate the fact that we were considering total system issues of Who-How-What. Too often organization concerns stop after What

How and forget the need to include the person issues—Who. Similarly, many individuals on their independence or ego trips never get beyond Who-How to the reality of the organization's What— RESULTS.

ACCOUNTABILITY FOR RESULTS

Our approach to applying the concept of Management by Objectives is to work toward achieving more effective organization RESULTS. We think this needs to be accomplished within a framework of accountability and interpersonal competence.

Accountability in many organizations is focused on individual task or activity accomplishment which, certainly, has value. However, these accomplishments do not necessarily produce organization RESULTS. A commitment to organization effectiveness means we consciously put the primary focus on organization RESULTS. In this context there is a much greater need for accountability relative to performance.

Past experience has validated the need for behavioral and interpersonal skills to be able to make MBO/R work. Many organizations have developed skills in objective writing, but have been unable or unwilling to move into a full system application. The first six chapters of this book will examine many different issues that we think are essential to making such an application. Chapters 7 through 16 are concerned with the methodology for making MBO/R work.

NOTES

1. The assumptions of Theory X and Theory Y are presented on pages 147 and 148 and discussed in various readings in Chapter 4 of our earlier book (1972): *A practical approach to organization development through MBO—selected readings.* Reading, Mass.: Addison-Wesley.

2. Gerard F. Carvalho 1973. *Critical issues in MBO*. A paper delivered to Mountain Plains Management Conference, Park City, Utah, (October) p. 2.

3. Robert A. Howell 1970. Managing by objectives: a three-stage system. *Business Horizons*, (February) pp. 42-43.

4. Harold M. F. Rush 1973. *Organization development: a reconnaissance.* New York: The Conference Board, p. 2.

5. Arthur C. Beck, Jr. and Ellis D. Hillmar 1972. OD to MBO or MBO to OD: Does it make a difference? *Personnel Journal,* (November) pp. 827-834.

VALUES AND THEIR EFFECT ON INDIVIDUALS AND ORGANIZATIONS

As we consider the various parts of a systemic approach to MBO/R, the subject of "values" may seem unusual. However, as we become increasingly conscious of the importance of the humanistic aspect in the goal setting process, individual and organizational values begin to have considerably more impact. Values and value systems provide direction to behavior and, therefore, will affect the implementation and application of MBO/R in an organization.

Though many people use the term values quite freely, our experience has been that relatively few people have a good under-standing of its full meaning and—more significantly—what *they* truly value. Through organizational research and human growth activities, there is increasing awareness of the significance of the values issue.

"Values are normative views held by individual human beings (consciously or subconsciously) of what is good and desirable. They provide standards by which people are influenced in their choice of actions. Social values reflect a system of shared beliefs which serve as norms of human conduct."[1] Values are the basis for deciding what one is for or against or where one is going and why. Values give direction to our lives and help to establish our character. They have to do with our "basic" or "core" ways of behaving as we are in rela-tionship with others and our environment. From only a few dozen basic values our various attitudes and beliefs flow out and are ex-perienced as actions relative to some subject, issue, or situation.[2]

Values evolve from one's life experiences and reflect many factors that come from our early family life, education, social level, community attitudes, etc. Thus, each individual has a unique combination that causes certain behavioral responses. When these are applied to management situations we find that personal values are important determinants in the choice of organization strategies.[3]

GETTING IN TOUCH WITH YOUR VALUES

In recent years our society has been confronted and placed under stress by significant pressures for change. In this turmoil, long accepted values have often been devastated leaving individuals and large segments of our adult population in bewilderment. Because of our growth in technology and as human beings we now have a much greater variety of alternatives from which to choose. This is a decision-making experience that is part of personal growth and having more freedom.

As more and more people, both young and old, have been "cut loose" from traditional values or roles, they have had to deal with many issues in life that were previously taken for granted or prescribed for them. Typical values areas are work, marriage, sex, politics, religion, leisure, money, time, life-style, and environment. These issues are not new, but changing patterns of behavior and technology are forcing us to deal with them in significantly different ways.

There is considerable personal gain in being more aware of what values are really strong for you because they are the essence of your own identity. This allows you to cope more adequately with your reality in the "now" situation without simply relying on "rights" or "wrongs" that have evolved from past experiences. However, the sometimes frightening aspect of this is that you must take on more responsibility *and* accountability for your own behavior since you are letting go of the traditions of the past. Managers need to develop more skill in coping with these new pressures and dilemmas.

Over the last twenty years (roughly the life of Management by Objectives) there has been a significant increase in humanistic concerns. "Who am I?" has emerged as a serious concern and search effort for many individuals. Such introspection and searching is viewed by most psychologists as a positive movement in personal growth because it develops a responsible view of one's self-worth. Much of the literature in this area identifies "I'm OK" feelings as an essential basic need for future effectiveness in organizational activities.[4] The popularity and success of Transactional Analysis (TA) is an indication of the desire for simple yet clear insights and understandings about one's self and one's behavior in organizations.[5]

Inherent in such growth activities is the reality of getting in touch with your values either directly or indirectly. Developing such values-awareness by examining the process of valuing helps us to identify what we value, where there are conflicts, how to differentiate in view of the changes that we are experiencing, and how to creatively cope with the responsible management of differences.

Valuing in this context is composed of choosing, prizing, and acting with these subprocesses:[6]

Choosing one's beliefs and behaviors

1. freely
2. from alternatives
3. after thoughtful consideration of the consequences of each alternative

Prizing one's beliefs and behaviors

4. cherishing, being happy with the choice
5. willing to affirm the choice publicly

Acting on one's beliefs

6. doing something with the choice
7. repeatedly, in some pattern of life

Much work has been done in developing values clarification workshops and techniques for teachers and students by Simon, Howe, and Kirschenbaum.[7] These learning experiences are equally appropriate, with little or no modification, for use by individuals.

Research on the subject has led to the understanding that an individual's values (attitudes and beliefs) come together in certain groupings, patterns, or systems. These data help to predict certain behaviors based on the predisposition to act in accordance with the values held. When working with an awareness of values, such groupings may be helpful in examining the "potency" of a given value. Some values are intense, basic, core items which are very strongly held whereas others are more representative of a belief or philosophical preference and therefore are more flexible in application.

A basic understanding of the relationship between values and goals is covered in this quotation from *The Futurist:*

> Needs determine values; and values determine goals. At any given level we tend to value what we need. If we are operating at the level of physiological needs, then we tend to value food and shelter. Attaining them becomes our goal. At the self-actualization level, we will be "turned on" by opportunities for self-expression, self-development, outreach. It is not, of course, that we need food, shelter, or any of the other intermediate needs any the less; but they are assumed or subsumed in the larger goal, rather than values for themselves. [8]

In this context, "needs" are identified with Abraham Maslow's five-level hierarchy of man's basic needs.[9] Thus, values will be generated in response to one's growth position in the hierarchy and certain goal-directed behavior will follow in an effort to satisfy the need. This is why we have come to view personal values and personal goal setting to be so important in the total process of MBO/R. This approach demands recognition of the reality of the human side—the Who aspect—of management. Working within a framework of increased alternatives requires greater clarity relative to the individual's values. Then the individual can cope more effectively with differences and conflicts while establishing personal goals which will lead to the satisfaction of personal needs within those organizations in which the person functions.

THE IMPACT OF VALUES ON THE ORGANIZATION

It is our belief that most organizations do not have a clearly established value system. When individuals come together, their values begin to interact and certain norms begin to emerge. But because organization values are not clearly stated, considerable energy is expended in conflict or in seeking to identify what values are operational. Typical areas in which organization values might be clarified are:

social issues	rewards
profitability	discipline
management style	control
conflict	power
openness	ethical issues
growth and change	competitiveness

When an organization begins to work with Organization Development there is greater likelihood that at least some of these issues will be worked since some form of clarification is a typical intervention.

Organization values have considerable impact on making MBO/R work. As covered above goals and objectives are set based on values while seeking to satisfy needs. We believe this to be equally appropriate for organizational and individual situations. If the needs and values are not clarified, many ineffective or inappropriate goals may be set.

As explained in Chapters 7 and 8 the first step in our approach to MBO/R is to develop a RESULT-oriented statement of the organization's mission. A clear understanding of values makes this a much easier process. Consider a hospital as an example of the variety of value systems which need to be integrated: patients, nurses, doctors, administrative staff, maintenance staff, board of directors, and various community groups including a number of volunteer organizations. To these add value issues relative to possible functions of teaching, patient care, research, and community medical service. At this point you have an extremely complex organizational environment in which to seek to implement a goal setting process. By working on values clarification at the total organization level, we begin to develop the "navigation system" (see Chapter 7) which allows subgroups and individuals to achieve an integration of their various contributions toward organization RESULTS.

Another aspect of developing values awareness and understanding the impact of values on organization life is emerging from work being done by Scott and Susan Myers as described in the article at the end of this chapter. They have developed a questionnaire (Values for Working) which provides an individual with a value system profile based on research by Clare Graves.[10] This approach uses hierarchical levels somewhat similar to Maslow's, but provides more descriptive behavioral data which allows for easier identification of various growth conditions. This research was applied at Texas Instruments (TI) and has provided some interesting insights into a variety of management and OD issues as documented in several articles by Flowers and Hughes.[11]

Emerging from the research and application at TI is a conclusion which is particularly relevant to making MBO/R work. The data suggests that an organization needs to have a very flexible MBO/R system. In this view, individuals at each level of existence should have an approach that meets their particular needs for maximum effectiveness within the organization. Thus, a given organization needs to have a general system that is flexible enough to provide a directive and structured application as well as a participative, free-flowing one.

As individuals and organizations develop a greater consciousness relative to their values, the management process can yield greater managerial effectiveness for the energy of the organization can be directed more clearly toward producing RESULTS. Values clarification facilitates the management of differences as part of a problem solving approach within the group process. This tends to provide for the fullest realization of the potential of the organization's human resources by satisfying human needs while producing organization RESULTS.

NOTES

1. F. E. Kast and J. E. Rosenzweig 1974. *Organization and management: a systems approach.* New York: McGraw-Hill, pp. 154-155.

2. For further reading on individual and organizational implications see also A.W. Mankoff 1974. Values—not attitudes—are the real key to motivation. *Management Review* (December) pp. 23-29.

3. W..D. Guth and R. Tagiuri 1965. Personal values and corporate strategy, *Harvard Business Review* (September-October), pp. 123-132.

4. See Talbot's article in Chapter 3 for additional understanding of the effect of "I'm OK" or "I'm not OK" feelings.

5. Suggested readings on the topic of TA: M. James and D. Jongeward 1971. *Born to win: transactional analysis with gestalt experiments*, Addison-Wesley; and J. Meininger 1973. *Success through transactional analysis*, Grosset and Dunlop.

6. L. E. Raths, M. Harmin, and S. B. Simon 1966. *Values and teaching*. Columbus, Ohio: Merrill, pp. 28-30.

7. S. B. Simon, L. W. Howe, and H. Kirschenbaum 1972. *Values clarification*. New York: Hart.

8. J.H. Wilson 1971. The new reformation (changing values and institutional goals), *The Futurist* (June), p. 157.

9. Maslow's hierarchy is briefly described on pages 150-151 of our earlier book (1972): *A practical approach to organization development through MBO—selected readings*. Reading, Mass.: Addision-Wesley.

10. *Ibid.*, pp. 168-181.

11. V. S. Flowers and C. L. Hughes 1973. Why employees stay, *Harvard Business Review*, (July-August) 1973, pp. 49-60.

_____, and B. A. Coda 1974. Human resource planning: foundation for a model, *Personnel* (January-February), pp. 20-42.

C.L. Hughes and V.S. Flowers 1973. Shaping personnel strategies to disparate value systems, *Personnel* (March-April), pp. 8-23.

_____. New goals in personnel, *Management by Objectives*, 3, 4, pp. 17-28.

ADAPTING TO THE NEW WORK ETHIC*

M. SCOTT MYERS AND SUSAN S. MYERS

Do you "see red" when a long-haired man walks into your office? Are there some "ungrateful wretches" in your organization who don't appreciate what the company is doing for them? What's

*We are indebted to Professor Clare W. Graves for providing the framework for this research and for critiquing the manuscript.
Reprinted by permission of the publisher from *The Business Quarterly* (Winter) 1973. © 1973 School of Business Administration, the University of Western Ontario, London, Canada.

wrong with people today who don't do what they're told to do? Whatever happened to company loyalty?

As organizational psychologists, we are finding supervisory problems to be symptoms of clashing or poorly understood value systems. A supervisor in a production department expressed it this way:

> People here aren't what they used to be. Several years ago most of our employees had WASP (White, Anglo-Saxon, Protestant) values. They were ambitious, conscientious, hard-working and honest, and you could count on them to get the job done. It was relatively easy to supervise this kind of person.
>
> We still have some of these, but now we're getting some different types who are difficult to supervise. Some are hippies who are bright enough, but their ideas are far-out, and they don't seem to care about pay, job security, or recognition from their supervisor.
>
> At the other extreme is a trouble-maker or free-loader type who isn't interested in the quantity or quality of work and is frequently absent or tardy. Some of them seem to look for opportunities to break the rules and will lie, cheat, and steal. Many of these come from the ghetto.

This supervisor's lament is echoed by those who apply traditional supervisory methods to people of the new work ethic. The problem is not restricted to business organizations, but is encountered in all walks of life. Parents and teachers are sometimes distressed by the appearance and behavior of young people. Clergymen are finding more concern with the here-and-now than in the hereafter, and government officials are encountering increasing rebellion against bureaucratic constraints. Union leaders are losing control of their members, and athletic coaches are learning that Lombardi-like charisma and domination no longer assure obedience and commitment among athletes. Some managers see these problems as symptoms of illness in society. A board chairman of a billion-dollar corporation cited as a sign of deteriorating values the inability of small local art shop manager to hire and retain young people. Noting that the pay was adequate and the work not unin teresting, he suggested that perhaps exposure to a severe economic depression might help realign their values.

This article provides a framework for understanding this problem, and defines some practical guidelines for organizational behavior, climate, and systems appropriate for people of today's values.

VALUES—OLD AND NEW

Based on 16 years of observation and research, Professor Graves* of Union College found that people seem to evolve through consecutive levels of "psychological existence" which are descriptive of personal values and life styles. Relatively independent of intelligence, a person's level of psychological existence can become arrested at a given level or it can move upward or downward depending on that person's cultural conditioning and his perception of the opportunities and constraints in his environment.

A diagramatic version of Graves's framework is presented in Exhibit I. The single-term label used at each stage of existence inadequately describes the syndrome it represents, but is used for convenience of discussion.

Level I. The *reactive* level of existence is most commonly observed in newborn babies or in people psychologically arrested in, or regressed to, infancy. They are unaware of themselves or others as human beings, and simply react to hunger, thirst, urination, defecation, sex, and other periodic physiological stimuli. Few people remain at this stage as they move toward adulthood; however, those at the threshold of subsistence in some of the larger cities of the Middle East seem to be little beyond this stage of existence. People at this level are generally not found on payrolls of organizations.

Level 2. Most people, as a matter of course, move out of the reactive existence to a *tribalistic* stage. Tribalism is characterized by concern with feelings of pain, temperature control, safety, and by tacit submission to an authority figure, whether he be a supervisor, policeman, government official, teacher, priest, parent, big brother

*Clare W. Graves 1970. Levels of existence: an open system theory of values. *Journal of Humanistic Psychology* (Fall) 10, 2:131–155.

EXISTENTIAL

High tolerance for ambiguity and people with differing values. Likes to do jobs in his own way without constraints of authority or bureaucracy. Goal oriented but toward a broader arena and longer time perspective.

MANIPULATIVE

Ambitious to achieve higher status and recognition. Strives to manipulate people and things. May achieve goals through gamesmanship, persuasion, bribery or official authority.

EGOCENTRIC

Rugged individualism, selfish, thoughtless, unscrupulous, dishonest. Has not learned to function within the constraints imposed by society. Responds primarily to power.

REACTIVE

Not aware of self or others as individuals or human beings. Reacts to basic physiological needs. Mostly restricted to infants.

SOCIOCENTRIC

High affiliation needs. Dislikes violence, conformity, materialism and manipulative management. Concerned with social issues and the dignity of man.

CONFORMIST

Low tolerance for ambiguity and for people whose values differ from his own. Attracted to rigidly defined roles in accounting, engineering, military, and tends to perpetuate the status quo. Motivated by a cause, philosophy, or religion.

TRIBALISTIC

Found mostly in primitive societies and ghettos. Lives in a world of magic, witchcraft and superstition. Strongly influenced by tradition and the power exerted by the boss, tribal chieftain, policeman, schoolteacher, politician, and other authority figures.

Exhibit I Levels of psychological existence.

or gang leader. Tribalism is commonly observed in primitive cultures where magic, witchcraft, ritual, and superstition prevail. For example, the Bantu who work in the coal, gold, and diamond mines of South Africa are largely tribalistic. Man at this level is locked into the rigid traditions of his tribe, and he is dominated by the tribal chieftain or his substitute.

Level 3. Egocentrism is an overly assertive form of rugged individualism. This person's behavior reflects a philosophy which seems to say, "To hell with the rest of the world. I'm for myself." He, or she, is typically premoral—thus unscrupulous, selfish, aggressive, restless, impulsive and, in general, not psychologically inclined to live within the constraints imposed by society's moral precepts. To this person, might is right, and authoritarian management, preferably benevolent, seems necessary to keep him in line. Typical group techniques are not usually successful for this type of person, but structured participative management, properly administered, promises to be an effective strategy for getting him out of this egocentric mode.

Both egocentrism and tribalism are found in U.S. ghettos—not as a function of ethnic determinants, but rather as a result of cultural disadvantage. Now that equal opportunity laws are accelerating the employment of minority people, egocentric and tribalistic behavior is more prevalent in organizations.

Level 4. Persons at the *conformity* level of existence have low tolerance for ambiguity, have difficulty in accepting people whose values differ from their own, and have a need to get others to accept their values. They usually subordinate themselves to a philosophy, cause, or religion, and tend to be attracted to vocations circumscribed by dogma or clearly defined rules. Though often perceived as docile, the conformist will assert or sacrifice himself in violence if his values are threatened. For example, in 1954, the normally law-abiding Archie Bunkers of Little Rock, Arkansas, erupted in violence against equal opportunity measures which violated the predominant value system of that region. Conformists prefer authoritarianism to autonomy, but will respond to participation if it is prescribed by an acceptable authority, and if it does not violate deep-seated values. They like specific job descriptions and procedures, and have little tolerance for supervisory indecision or weakness. People at this level have been the mainstay of the hourly work force since the beginning of the Industrial Revolution.

Level 5. The fifth level of psychological existence is characterized by *manipulative* or materialistic behavior. Persons at this level are typically products of the Horatio Alger, rags-to-riches philosophy— striving to achieve their goals through the manipulation of things and people within their environment. They thrive on gamesmanship, politics, competition, and entrepreneurial effort, measure their success in terms of materialistic gain and power, and are inclined to flaunt self-earned (as against hereditary) status symbols. Typical of level 5 persons are business managers, who define their goals and strategies in terms such as cash flow, return on investment, profits, share of the market and net sales billed, and their focus is generally on short-term targets such as the quarterly review or annual plan. They tend to perceive people as expense items rather than assets, to be manipulated as supplies and equipment.

Level 6. People at the sixth, or *sociocentric*, level of existence have high affiliation needs. Getting along is more important than getting ahead, and the approval of people they respect is valued over individual fame. At this level he may return to religiousness, not for its ritual or dogma, but rather for its spiritual attitude and concern with social issues. Many members of the original "hippie" cult were sociocentrics—their hirsute and dungareed appearance being a symbolic put-down of the organization-man appearance approved by the establishment. On the job the sociocentric responds well to participative management, but only on the condition that he and the others he values believe in his product or service. He tends to articulate his protests openly, but characteristically dislikes violence and would counter authoritarianism with passive resistance. Sociocentrics are frequently perceived as cop-outs by 4s and 5s, and their behavior is not generally rewarded in business organizations. As a result, persons at this level who do not ultimately capitulate by regressing to the organizationally accepted modes of manipulation and conformity, or adapt by evolving to the seventh level of psychological existence, may become organizational problems because of alcoholism, drug abuse, or other self-punitive behavior.

Level 7. The individual at the *existential* level of existence has high tolerance for ambiguity, and for persons whose values differ from his own. On the job his behavior might say, "O.K., I understand the job to be done—now leave me alone and let me do it my way." In some respects he is a blend of levels 5 and 6 in that he is goal-oriented toward organizational success (level 5) and concerned with the dignity of his fellowman (level 6). Like the level 5, he is concerned with organizational profits, the quarterly review, and the annual plan, but he is also concerned with the ten-year or fifty-year plan and the impact of the organization on its members, the community and the environment. Like the level 6, he is repelled by the use of violence. However, his outspoken intolerance of inflexible systems, restrictive policy, status symbols, and the arbitrary use of authority is threatening to most level 4 and 5 managers, and he may be expelled from the organization for reasons of nonconformity or insubordination.

Most people in today's organizations can be described in terms of levels 2 through 7. Though level 7 is not the ultimate level of development, models for higher levels are sufficiently scarce to make their definition difficult and, for the purpose of this paper, unnecessary.

MEASURING VALUES IN THE BUSINESS ORGANIZATION

Seeing in Graves' theory a possible explanation for many organizational problems, we chose this framework for analyzing the problem of disparate values in organizations. The first step was to develop and standardize a questionnaire* for measuring levels of psychological existence and for determining the extent to which the various levels are represented in the business organization. The Values for Working questionnaire consists of 18 job and employment-oriented types of items, such as systems and procedures, job descriptions,

*M.S. Myers and S.S. Myers, *Values for working.* © 1973, Dallas, Texas.

benefits, career development, and supervision. Each multiple-choice item was developed and refined so that each of its six responses correlated most significantly with the factor it was intended to represent. For example, in the following item about Boss, these relationships are expressed as correlation coefficients:

The kind of boss I like is one who	Correlation Coefficients					
	T	E	C	M	S	X
a — calls the shots and isn't always changing his mind, and sees to it that everyone follows the rules.	20	-00	44	01	-17	-28
b — gives me access to the information I need and lets me do my job in my own way.	-28	-33	-27	-29	11	46
c — tells me exactly what to do and how to do it, and encourages me by doing it with me.	26	11	19	04	06	-12
d — doesn't ask questions as long as I get the job done.	13	15	01	28	-12	-24
e — gets us working together in close harmony by being more a friendly person than a boss.	01	12	-15	00	32	-13
f — is tough but allows me to be tough too.	06	33	17	19	-26	-13

IMPLICATIONS FOR MANAGEMENT

Data collected from salaried exempt persons comprise norms for making subgroup comparisons. Sources of potential conflict are revealed in Exhibit II which shows actual value profiles (not necessarily typical) of individuals in various levels and functions in industry.

For example, Profile A represents a conservative president

(solid line) and one of his vice-presidents (broken line), who left the company to become president of another organization. The vice-president, with his greater need for independence, higher tolerance for people of differing values, and lower conformity needs, clashed with the more egocentric and highly conforming president who had little tolerance for people whose views differed from his own.

The profile of the new president offers better potential for the development of free thinking and inner-directed vice-presidents than that of his former boss. The senior president's role, in practice, is similar to that of an overprotecting parent who has high expectations of his children, arbitrarily dispensing rewards and punishments, and developing dependency relationships. But the president is only perpetuating values which he was rewarded for possessing by his dynamic board chairman boss.

Knowing that the chairman dislikes yes-men, these high-level yes-men have learned how to protest in an acceptable fashion. For example, on one occasion the president pounded the table during a board meeting in exaggerated protest to the chairman's perceptive allegation that managerial dereliction was a cause of the unionization of a plant and that other union penetrations were imminent. The president asserted loudly that unionization of the one plant was caused by forces beyond the control of the company and that until the other plants were, in fact, unionized, such an accusation was only speculation. However, the board chairman's concern with unionization touched off a manipulative anti-union strategy far more costly than preventive measures would have been. But the tablepounding in the board room probably served to show the chairman that he was not surrounded by docile conformists.

In a young organization, independent, entrepreneurial types come to the top. But, as success is achieved, these early risk-takers become more conservative and intolerant of the very type of behavior that enabled them to succeed. Ambitious managers on the way up have a choice of leaving the organization, asserting their initiative under a facade of conformity, or acquiescing to puppetry. Under this style of leadership, conformity-oriented managers are promoted.

Profile B in Exhibit II is a vice-president in an organization that is beginning to show signs of hardening of the arteries. His higher conformity, sociocentric and tribalistic profile and lower

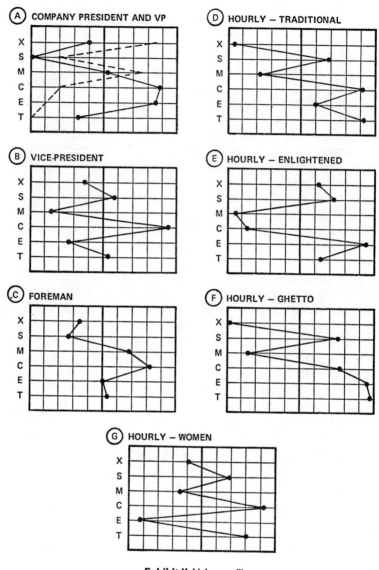

Exhibit II Value profiles.

manipulative, egocentric, and existential scores are descriptive of a person who seeks to please the boss, perpetuate tradition and avoid rocking the boat. Frequently prefacing his directives to his subordinates with "Now what I believe Max (president) wants is . . ." or "Max is quite concerned (for example) with blocked growth opportunities in the company, therefore, we should be collecting data to shed light on this problem—just in case he asks for it"; he is more concerned with anticipating the boss's whims than he is with the real problem facing the organization. Sometimes a simple and innocent observation or question by the president is transformed and amplified by this conformist zealot into a high priority and arbitrary edict. Though it is the vice-president's interpretations that are in error, it is the president's fault for having nurtured conformity behavior.

The foreman's high conformity and manipulative profile (C) is typical of the person who has been promoted from the ranks, and is ideal for evoking and perpetuating conformity behavior among the traditional hourly ranks (D). Though the high egocentric score of the traditional hourly reflects self-centered opportunism, it is strongly counterbalanced by high tribalistic, conformity, and sociocentric scores. In other words, this person needs to protect his self-esteem by following a strong and respected leader, clearly defined rules, and group acceptance, rather than take the risk of striking out on his own.

The "enlightened hourly" employee (E) tends to be younger, better informed, concerned with social issues, idealistic, and somewhat antiestablishment in his views. Potentially this more enlightened person would not have the high egocentric score shown here. This regression to lower level values typically occurs when this type of person finds himself boxed in by inappropriate management, as would come from foreman C. Often restless and unwilling to adjust to automaton conformity, he has the ability to view life in perspective, and recoils at the thought of 30 years of monotony climaxed by retirement with a gold watch. Though their educational backgrounds range from college dropouts to little formal education, most enlightened hourlies have acquired much information (selectively assimilated) from television, travel, and social interaction. They respond best to a supervisor who respects them, asks for and uses their ideas, and gives them freedom to socialize and manage a job.

The foreman also encounters problems in dealing with the culturally disadvantaged from the ghetto (F), whose high egocentrism-

tribalism combination often focuses their conforming and sociali-
zing activities toward peer group rebellion against the organization.
Egocentrics are against the world in general and, if he's black,
against "whitey" in particular. Hence, the white supervisor, regard-
less of his qualifications, has little opportunity to succeed with black
egocentrics. The black supervisor, on the other hand, can impose
supervisory constraints in the language of the ghetto, avoiding
allegations of racial discrimination. However, experience has shown
that one level of black supervision is not enough—it is often perceived as tokenism or "Uncle-Tomism." But if at least two levels of
black supervision exist in the organization (for example, foreman
and superintendent), a new message comes through to the black
egocentric that "this is my organization too, and I and my people
can succeed here." If two or more levels of black supervision exist in
the organization, the white supervisor can successfully supervise
blacks, as long as blacks are also supervising whites. This principle
is not restricted to black-white relationships, but applies wherever
occupational discrimination occurs; for example, such as once
existed between the English- and French-speaking Canadians in the
Province of Quebec, or between men and women in most organizations.

Profile G is typical for hourly paid women. Their highs in 2, 4,
and 6, and lows in 3, 5, and 7, reflect their cultural conditioning to
be friendly, loyal, and obedient followers. Reinforced by tradition,
women have been rewarded for performing support roles, both in
the home and at the work place. Thus, they can be found in large
numbers on assembly lines, behind typewriters, in libraries, at telephone switchboards, and at keypunch machines—but not in board
rooms or offices—unless they are serving the coffee. It is interesting
to note, however, the similarity between their profile (G) and that of
the vice-president in profile B.

LEVEL 4 AND 5 PROTOTYPES

Conservative or manipulative managers, who tend to dominate most
organizations, typically engage in defensive strategies ranging from
pretending a problem doesn't exist, through adopting more restrictive personnel selection criteria, to attempting to reshape the values
of the "misfits" now on the work force.

A manager from a large manufacturing organization deplored the disappearance of what he referred to as the old-style, dynamic leaders like Vince Lombardi. "What we need in our organization," he said, "is a lot of Vince Lombardis—leaders who will drive through and achieve organizational objectives," not realizing that Lombardi's leadership, effective for coaching a football team in the 60s, may be inappropriate for today's business organization. In the first place, his style of leadership tends to overshadow the talent in the organization, creating little opportunity for the development of subordinates. For instance, none of the coaches that served under Lombardi succeeded in emulating his success as a result of his tutelage. Furthermore, there is room for only one Lombardi in an organization, as he calls all the shots; but a business organization has many interdependent functions to be managed through the cooperation of many able leaders. When the Lombardi-type person leaves, the organization tends to lose its effectiveness because of the dependency relationships fostered by his personality.

Lombardi's life-style most closely fits the pattern of a level 4. For example, he was a faithful churchgoer, he dictated the life-styles of his players, and reinforced his values by replaying a recording of an evangelistic West Point speech about love, honor, and duty by Douglas MacArthur, one of his heroes. Most level 4 people need heroes, just as they, in turn, need to be heroes and need to dominate people in their organization. This is not a criticism of Lombardi; his success as a football coach speaks for itself. But, it is a criticism of this style of leadership for organizations in which increasing numbers are above the 2, 3, and 4 levels of psychological existence.

Managers are not only culturally conditioned by the tradition of 5 and 4 style management but they are also influenced by persons outside the organization whose values can affect the organization's status. Market analysts, for example, will respond positively to a layoff that will improve the cost-earnings ratio in a way that increases stock prices. Hence, short-range 4 and 5 thinking by analysts inspires and perpetuates 4 and 5 management strategies in organizations.

Of course, some of the level 4 and 5 influence may come more directly from the manager's wife and other members of his family. Women, long conditioned to conservative support roles or defensively skilled in manipulation, often exert subtle but significant influences on the life-style of the manager. However, in many cases, the wives and children are also serving as bridges between industry and society, providing a counterbalancing influence to the organization by sensitizing managers to sociocentric and existential concepts.

GUIDELINES FOR COMPATIBILITY

In spite of their conditioned high regard for Lombardi-like leadership, managers are, with increasing frequency, finding themselves out of step with the people they supervise. Conformity behavior, once taken for granted, can no longer be expected. Not only are the managers out of step, but so are many of the systems which they use to achieve organizational goals. Since systems reflect the values of their designers and administrators, it is only natural to find people responding to systems as they do to the managers who create and administer them. Exhibit III presents capsule descriptions of supervisory values, systems characteristics, and subordinate or systems user values.

The three left columns of Exhibit III show characteristic supervisory (S) attitudes toward subordinates at levels 2 through 7 as they relate to the supervisory functions of performance review, communication and career planning. Immediately beneath the supervisor's value statement at each level is shown a characteristic value statement for supervised employees (E) at that level.

The right side of Exhibit III contains descriptors and values relating to three personnel management systems—compensation, attitude survey, and job posting. At each level is a capsule descriptor of the system (S) as it might characteristically be conceived by a system designer at that level of psychological existence. Immediately beneath each descriptor is summarized an expectation of the system as it might characteristically be expressed by an employee (E) at that level.

This table identifies conditions of compatibility and conflict within the organization. For example, in considering the "communication" relationships, the level 7 supervisor's view (We discuss things informally, and I give them access to any information they want), is compatible with the needs of the 7s, 6s, and 5s he supervises:

7: I like to feel free to talk to anyone, and to get the information I want.

6: He's easy to talk to and is interested in us personally.

5: If I'm to do a good job, I need to know everything my boss knows.

However, in reading farther down the column it becomes apparent that the needs of the 4s, 3s and 2s are less compatible:

4: He should tell us what we're supposed to know to do our job properly.

3: The less I hear from my boss, the better.

2: He tells us what to do in a friendly way and lets us know he'll help us.

The 4s and 2s want more structure, and the 3s need more structure than the 7 would naturally provide.

However, the actual situation in organizations is more serious than the partial incompatibility reflected in the example above. Managers are typically more 5 or 4 than 7 in their orientation and, consequently, encounter more conflict. For example, the level 5 supervisor's communication philosophy (I give them the information I think they need to get the job done) is not easily compatible with any level except 4 (He should tell us what we're supposed to know to do our job properly). This means that level 5, the most common type of leadership style, has little opportunity to succeed unless he surrounds himself with conformists. In the long run, he and the organization would, of course, be defeated by excessive conformity.

The same phenomenon exists regarding the compatibility of people and management systems. Compensation, attitude survey, and job-posting systems designed in terms of level 7 concepts are compatible with 7, 6, and 5 values, but not with 4, 3, and 2 values. Since most systems are designed in terms of level 4 and 5 concepts, they tend to satisfy the 2, 3, and 4 levels and frustrate people at the 5, 6, and 7 levels. In other words, systems in most organizations are

		SUPERVISION			SYSTEMS		
---	---	PERFORMANCE REVIEW	COMMUNICATION	CAREER PLANNING	COMPENSATION	ATTITUDE SURVEY	JOB POSTING
7	S	We work together in setting goals and reviewing progress.	We discuss things informally, and I give them access to any information they want.	Self-development is the key; people should have the opportunity to plan their own careers.	A smorgasbord approach which rewards merit and adapts to individual needs.	A democratic process involving all people in analyzing problems and suggesting improvements.	A system for maximizing organizational effectiveness by encouraging the natural flow of talent.
	E	I like to have a major role in defining my goals and methods for achieving them.	I like to feel free to talk to anyone, and to get the information I want.	I am responsible for my own career, and require the opportunity to develop my capabilities.	A good system rewards merit and doesn't tie you to the organization.	Greater commitment and solidarity are achieved when people have a hand in solving problems.	Now that I know what the openings and requirements are, I can run my own maze.
6	S	I try to review their performance without hurting their feelings.	I want to be on good terms with them so they will feel they can discuss anything with me.	Every career should include the ingredients of social and civic responsibility.	Pay and benefits tailored to the needs of the people and their circumstances.	A vehicle for diagnosing and solving human problems.	A system providing opportunity for employees to find compatible work groups and supervisors.
	E	He should use this occasion to get better acquainted with us.	He's easy to talk to and is interested in us personally.	Our careers should be oriented toward bettering relationships among all people.	Money should serve all people, and be more equitably distributed.	Working with others in analyzing survey results is a good way to improve human relations.	I like being able to find a job where the people and work don't clash with my values.
5	S	I find that the carrot and stick works best.	I give them the information I think they need to get the job done.	I keep track of their progress and specify developmental programs and assignments.	Distribution of money according to amount of responsibility and level of performance.	A management tool for taking the pulse of an organization.	A controlled, competitive system to upgrade the best employees into company job openings.
	E	I like to set my own goals and get recognition for achieving them.	If I'm to do a good job, I need to know everything my boss knows.	My career depends on my taking the initiative in finding opportunity for advancement.	Money is a measure of my success.	If what we learn from an attitude survey can make our employees more productive, I'm all for it.	It's one way to find advancement opportunities, but it helps to know the right people.

4 S	I define the goals and standards I expect them to follow.	I give them the information they should have, and keep our relations businesslike.	I define their career paths and promotional opportunities and give them continuous guidance.	Compensation programs based on community and industry surveys and standard practice.	The systematic measurement of attitudes toward company goals, policies and practices.	The orderly, systematic and fair implementation of a promotion-from-within policy.
E	We need to know the company goals and how we can support them.	He should tell us what we're supposed to know to do our job properly.	I will be promoted when I earn it through productiveness and loyalty.	Money is a reward for loyalty and hard work, and should not be subject to favoritism.	Management is asking for our help, and it is our duty to answer all questions as honestly as possible.	I will be given the job I bid on if I deserve it.
3 S	I make clear what he has to do if he wants to keep his job.	I tell them whatever I feel like telling them.	It's every man for himself — don't look to me for your breaks.	Manipulative, arbitrary and secretive use of money.	Rigged questions and whitewashed reports.	Posting of jobs that can't be filled more economically from the outside.
E	I don't like anyone finding fault with me and telling me how to act.	The less I hear from my boss, the better.	I don't want anyone planning my life — I'll look after No. 1 myself.	I'll work for the highest bidder.	I don't want any part of a stool pigeon system that can be used against me.	It's no use trying — the cards are stacked against you.
2 S	I tell them how I think they did and how they can improve.	I explain company rules to them and talk with them about their problems.	They expect me to tell them what to do and to take care of them.	A fair and uniform system administered by the boss.	A way of letting employees know the company is interested in their ideas.	A way of increasing job security by filling job openings from within.
E	I want him to tell me if I've done what he wanted me to do, and if I've let him down.	He tells us what to do in a friendly way and lets us know he'll help us.	What's most important is that I'll always have a steady job and a good boss.	I need steady pay to make ends meet.	My boss should know how we feel so he can help us.	I'll bid on a job if my supervisor tells me to.

S (Supervisor System)
E (Employee)

Exhibit III Expectations and needs by value level.

designed more for people at the conformist, egocentric and tribalistic level than they are for the entrepreneurial self-starters in 5, 6, and 7. This stems in part from the fact that the job of systems and procedures writer is more likely to attract level 4 conformists than any other level. Hence, as a counter-balancing influence, level 7 criteria must be applied to remove the unnecessary and inflexible constraints typically reflected in policy and procedure statements.

CONCLUSIONS

The new work ethic is not a new set of values; rather, it represents a shift in the source of influence. The seven levels of psychological existence described in this paper have long existed, but people in the middle ranges of manipulation and conformity have, until recently, been the unchallenged source of influence in business organizations and in most realms of society for at least the past 600 years.

Now, thought-leaders are beginning to come as well from the existential and sociocentric levels. Though they still represent a minority, their values are permeating our culture at an accelerating rate. In business organizations, for example, pressures are being felt on many fronts. Corporate managers are beginning to forego promotional transfers to stay in the community of their choice. Some employees are refusing overtime or to work on implements of war. Others pressure their management to cease trade with South Africa. Union members are more interested in meaningful work than fatter benefits. Thus, neither management nor labor is immune to the influence of 6 and 7 thinking.

New thought-leaders are also surfacing issues which precipitate social, civic, and legislative action. It was largely level 5 interests that planned to host the 1976 Winter Olympics in Colorado, but it was apparently level 7 and 6 leadership (concerned with ecology and commercialism), coupled with level 4 conservatism, that defeated the effort at the polls. The 4s were probably always against exploitation of their area, but heretofore were not psychologically predisposed toward organizing opposition.

Women's liberation groups have initiated a number of reforms under level 7 leadership such as that of Aileen Hernandez. Their influence has reduced employment discrimination against women, changed abortion laws, opened vocational opportunities in restricted fields such as business, law, and medicine, and promises to secure legal implementation of the Equal Rights Amendment to the Constitution.

Though conformists still conform, they are beginning to emulate new models. For example, the mod look of the level 6 has become the conformity model of the level 4 in American society. People of other values adopt the new look, but for different reasons. Level 5s wear sideburns and variegated apparel when it is advantageous to do so, and level 7s may wear the new look simply because it suits their fancy. Level 3s wear anything that symbolizes independence, and 2s wear what their "tribal chieftains" expect them to wear.

Value conflicts that exist today are not resolved, of course, by simply adopting the mod clothing and language. They can be ameliorated only by learning to operate from a new source of influence. The level 4 or 5 manager tends to operate from influence derived from official authority and tradition. To succeed with the new work ethic, he must operate from a base of influence stemming from the competence of people at all levels of the organization. That is, he will be skilled in organizing manpower and material in such a way that human talent can find expression in solving problems and setting goals. He will know he is succeeding when the people stop fighting him, and show commitment in achieving job goals. Incidentally, when he reaches this level of competence, he will find that the person who has changed the most is himself—and he and the level 7s are now talking the same language.

EMPOWERMENT—DEVELOPING PERSONAL POWER TO SUPPORT AUTHORITY POWER

As consultants working with managers and organizations to implement MBO/R, we have frequently been confronted with the power issue as a barrier to implementation. Typically, a manager has just indicated how great MBO/R sounds and then discounts the enthusiasm with "...but my boss would never let me try that!" Or it comes through as "Why don't you sell this idea to them (upper management)? I can't do anything unless *they* say its OK." In reality, MBO/R is a process of change that has a high potential for creating considerable stress in an organization since it is likely to modify various power relationships.

Power is a word that is used often in management literature, yet there seems to be little understanding of its full meaning and constructive potential. When discussing power with managers—particularly those at lower levels in the organization—there is often considerable negativity or hostility. This attitude is generally supported by "war stories" about what happened in this power struggle or how that manager abused power. The moral of the story turns out to be, "Remember what happened to good old Joe; he got put on the shelf." Unfortunately, much of the folklore is true, and the subject of power is not a popular one.

Our approach has been to use a concept of emPOWERment[1] to establish a positive direction for the supportive use of authority and influence within the organization. It has proved to be useful in making MBO/R work. Many others have also found these ideas to be of considerable value in general management practice.

SOME THOUGHTS AND OBSERVATIONS ABOUT POWER

A significant aspect of the literature on power is that there is no common agreement on what power is. Philosophy, behavioral science, social science, management science, and the general literature each have their particular perspective, as do given authors within those fields. Generally, power is defined as the ability to control or influence what happens to both material and human resources in an organization. Management books often refer to French and Raven's five types of "social power": referent, expert, reward, coercive, and legitimate.[2] Or perhaps McClelland's "Need for Power" might be presented in relation to motivational drives.[3] The subject is normally dealt with at a high level of abstraction so that a working manager gets little "know-how" relative to applications issues.

Managerial power is difficult to deal with since it is never really "seen" by itself. Rather, it always manifests through some other form or the behavior of individuals. Perhaps the most common concept of power at the operating level is that related to authority and control which is referred to as the power of office or position. In this case, person A relies on some rule, law, agreement, or relationship to give the *authority* (often perceived as power) to get person B to do something. This tends to demand conformity and create a condition of dependency through control. It represents a very limited view of power and is more appropriately a function of authority which is called power.

Carvalho points out that ". . . there is a tendency for managers to hold the attitude that there is some absolute amount of power available to an organizational entity, and if some members of that organization acquire more power, it must be at the expense of previous power holders."[4] He then makes the point that power in an organization can be expanded, that it is not fixed and absolute. We are in agreement and use the process of emPOWERment to facilitate the expansion through the development of *personal* power. However, this means that we have to develop a different concept of power.

FOCUSING THE ENERGY THAT GIVES LIFE TO AN ORGANIZATION

Power is also defined as the capacity to act physically. Thus, we have a physical force moving or energy flowing. It is a scientific fact that energy can be produced by creating a different form and pattern of flow. Also, the less resistance there is in the system, the more energy flow and *power* you have available.

In applying these same concepts to an organization we are working with the emPOWERment of a human system. In our approach this power or energy flow gives life to an organization. Management's challenge is to focus that energy to produce RESULTS. Organizational direction for this power potential is provided through the goal setting process.

To apply this approach to emPOWERment, refer to Talbot's M-C-P Model (Fig. 3.1 and Table 1) for the basic understanding of how various issues relate and need to be managed to achieve the balance between authority and personal power. The dynamic thrust (energy flow) within the organization is moving from the individual (inclusion) toward organization RESULTS (outcomes). Some basic considerations in using this model would be:

- Differences, roles, norms, and structure are "behavioral" issues that must be worked and managed for clarity and agreement to achieve emPOWERment and RESULTS
- People-concern flows from inclusion towards outcomes
- Work-concern flows from outcomes towards inclusion
- Fundamental issues are Membership (Who), Control (How), and Production (What)
- As managers and individuals we must learn to "think (in terms of) systems" and be aware of the interrelatedness of Who-How-What. This will be discussed further in Chapter 6.

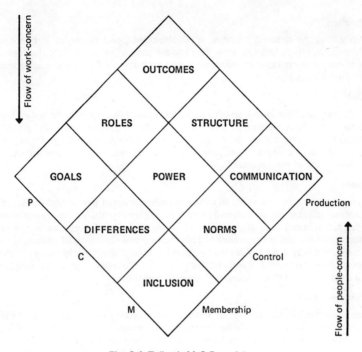

Fig. 3.1 Talbot's M-C-P model.

Table 1 Factor Descriptions for M-C-P Model

Outcomes

Outcomes are the end-results of task production which affect the organization's contribution to its environment, to its own self-maintenance, and to the people who serve in the organization. Outcomes are seen as internal and external, as tangible and qualitative, as rewards and punishments, as new potential and depletion, as transactions, and as values.

Roles

Roles are symbols which identify functions and clarify relationships between members and groups within an organization. Roles represent functions and relationships which are effectively more important to the organization than to individual members. Role development is the process of identifying particular relationships which individuals or groups have in performing various functions in an organization; it is clarified through human interaction, working directly with the feelings, attitudes, and behavioral relationships of the people involved.

Structure

Structure is the ordering together of people, power, and resources in bounded relationships which channel work flow toward productive goals. It is the formal identification of how the organization will do what it sets out to do, and how various parts work together.

Goals

Goals are the targets toward which purposeful activity in an organization is directed. To be useful, goals are time-structured, specific, feasible, measurable, and provide a basis for evaluation at some future point in time. They are the linking pins of purpose with the organization's environment, its internal maintenance, and the needs of the people in the organization.

Power

Power is the energy and ability to influence decisions about people and resources. Power is taken by use, and given by use, but not given by abdication. Power in an organization is not used alone, but is channeled through the vehicles of norms, roles, structure, and management of differences. Power is exercised personally by virtue of the way a person perceives himself in relationship to other persons and groups. Power is exercised authoritatively by virtue of holding a particular position in a structure to which organizational power is assigned.

Communication

Communication is the process of sending and receiving data which has understandable meaning to both sender and receiver. Communication is used to establish human relationships, to facilitate transactions, and to transmit information needed for control and production functions. Diagnostically, the quality of interpersonal communications is a behavioral statement of the quality of the human relationship.

Differences

The management of differences in resources, power, or people is the key process in productive or creative effort. Work is the functional use of differences and similarities. Conflict is the dysfunctional use of differences and similarities. Differences can also be managed by avoidance. Differential management focuses internally on the development and use of people, power and resources toward purposeful goals. It focuses externally on procurement of membership and resources, and the productive and distributive return to the environment.

Norms

Norms are the unwritten rules of group behavior (the informal structure) which are initiated and maintained by collective human behavior. These are influenced initially by the expectations, attitudes and assumptions which members bring to a group. A norm is feeling-oriented and sanctioned by consensus, as the result of real or implied behavior in groups. It is operative only as long as it is reinforced by further behavior or stands unchallenged by differing behavior. Norms can be perceived as restrictive or generative, according to their influence on the effective functioning of the organizations.

Inclusion

Inclusion is the process of building a relationship. It involves the feelings and behavior of people in the acceptance of similarities and differences, the building of give-receive relationships, and coping with the dynamics of acceptance and rejection.

THE POSITIVE USE OF EMPOWERMENT TO PRODUCE ORGANIZATION RESULTS

Until there is energy flowing, power merely has "potential"—as in a battery. Power must be taken by use. It may be taken as a "rip-off" when someone moves in and grabs it because no one is doing anything. Or it may be used more positively through this concept of emPOWERment. In using the process of emPOWERment we seek to open up the human (behavioral) system flow in a way that minimizes the power dilemma. We have emPOWERment in an organization when individuals are able to put their personal power together within an authority structure to produce organization RESULTS. This "win-win" approach is most functional within a supportive system of MBO/R since goals provide a strong cohesive force.

Part of the process of emPOWERment is resolving issues of inclusion within the organization. This also relates to the values discussion in Chapter 2. Values and emPOWERment come together in the development of a healthy self-concept which leads to personal and psychological growth. Our experience has been that unless these issues of emPOWERment are dealt with as part of the total goal setting process, objective writing will be a short-lived, paperwork exercise that is headed for failure. The M-C-P model supports this in that unless individuals are able to manage their own individuality and differences in their role situation, objectives won't move to the reality of performance outcomes.

NOTES

1. We are indebted to John C. Talbot, a management consultant in organization development, for much of our "theory" base on emPOWERment. At this time most of his work is unpublished, and we

are drawing on personal discussions and data presented in seminars conducted by him. This has been augmented by our own experience in working with the approach.

2. J.R.P. French, Jr. and B.H. Raven 1959. The bases of social power. In D. Cartwright (ed.), *Studies in social power.* Ann Arbor, Michigan: University of Michigan.

3. D.C. McClelland 1961. *The achieving society.* Princeton, N.J.: Van Nostrand.

4. G.F. Carvalho 1972. Installing management by objectives: a new perspective on organizational change. *Human Resource Management* **11**, 1, (Spring), p. 26.

THE DEVELOPMENT OF POWER RELATIONSHIPS IN MANAGEMENT

JOHN C. TALBOT

A central behavioral issue in many organizations is achieving an effective style for the use of power. Power is the ability to influence what happens to people and things in human organizations. The way power is used has considerable impact on the effectiveness of the results.

A clear distinction between authoritative power and personal power may be a helpful starting point. Authority is designated organizational power. *Authoritative power* is created through structured relationships in organizations. It is assigned, differentiated, and limited. It is exercised by virtue of occupying a designated role within the structure. *Personal power* is felt and owned from within oneself. It is directly related to how we see ourselves and how we perceive others. It is exercised through personal role relationships and ability to influence others. There is also a group dimension to personal power. All that we have said above can be applied to group consciousness and group activity as well. The goal is to use both authoritative and personal power together effectively. It often happens differently.

Many times different kinds of managers end up using these two types of power competitively against each other. Some managers may rely heavily upon authoritative power while other managers, because of their function or preference, rely principally upon personal power. It may get intensely competitive. For instance, the often-stereotyped line-staff relationship is an example. The line manager has fears: the other guy has real power (his own); mine can be taken away. The staff manager has fears: the other guy can wipe me out (history says it does happen).

The outcome of the competition is that the line manager becomes more coercive, exerts tighter authoritative control and plays avoidance/manipulation games (such as "Re-direct," "Twenty Questions," "Secret Management," "Memo," etc.) The outcome for the staff manager is the decision to keep a low profile and not own all his power. "Beat the System" is an appealing attack game. All games must be played carefully. The other guy's power is structurally reinforced and often exercised very impersonally. The end results are fear and frustration, wasted energy, and a win-lose position for both.

The advice comes easy:

- initiate working relationships on the basis of personal power, starting from a position of independence and building toward personal interdependence.
- identify and reject win-lose behavior.
- negotiate win-win working relationships.

The doing is often hard. It requires major changes in behavior and attitudes, both of which take time, effort, risk, and often the help of a third party facilitator.

ROOTS OF THE POWER ISSUE

The motivational roots of the power issue run deep in the dichotomy of authority and dependency. We need only to recall the all-too-familiar pattern of power/powerless relations between superiors and subordinates as an example. The superior and the subordinate both use power according to their perception of what is appropriate in the relationship. This may be extremely limited, or broad and flexible. Power in interpersonal relationships depends on how we perceive power in others, in ourselves, and in a combined relationship between others and ourselves. It is dynamic, changing. It is felt and acted on in behavior. It is very personal.

It is often useful to examine power relationships in management group life in the same way that these are viewed in personal development. The child begins life in a dependent relationship upon parents, social institutions, and other protective, directive, or didactic social relationships. Hopefully the little person grows through a series of relationships which increase his or her ability to choose and act, alone and in concert with others. The feelings and perceptions about oneself gradually change from being inferior, subordinate, dependent, and not OK to feelings of being acceptable, which includes acceptance of both the likeable and unlikeable aspects of self as OK, the internalizing and rebalancing of interpersonal power relationships, and development of competence to act alone and with others.

FOUR STAGES OF THE DEPENDENCY SYNDROME

The dependency syndrome is a series of perceptions and consequent behaviors which arise out of the value judgments we place on ourselves and others. It describes the mode of power relationships in any situation. People need people. The thing that matters is how they meet that need. A particular type of dependence may be functional and appropriate or dysfunctional and disruptive to the needed relationships. Growth in our ability to interact in power relationships with others moves through four stages, from *dependence* to *counterdependence* to *independence* to *interdependence*. All four modes of relationship are needed and useful in ongoing adult relationships.

A few quick illustrations:

The vice-president of marketing has asked his staff for an updated analysis of consumer trends. He is *dependent* on the expertise of others for this.

A manufacturing manager is probing the administrative budgets of his department heads for cost control. The behavior is *counterdependent* and applied toward the functional purpose of responsible budget management.

A senior manager of a large corporation staff group asks and encourages his work group to set their own yearly objectives, encouraging *independent* initiative and behavior.

The chief executive of an organization sits with his staff to review a long-range plan. The group is *interdependent*, unable to synthesize a good plan unless all parties contribute in ways congruent to their own expectations. To arrive at this point, he tests with his staff appropriate dependencies and interdependencies, engages in critical examination (counterdependence) and seeks to preserve independence of initiative in all of his staff. This is a thumbnail sketch of the functional uses of all modes of power relatedness.

THE STAGE OF DEPENDENCE

Dependence means literally "to hang down from." As a function, dependence means I must receive from another something which I need, whether it be care, nourishment, protection, knowledge, a specialized function, a service, or direction and sanction. For instance, I am dependent on a doctor to take out my appendix. It is quite appropriate to be dependent upon someone for something I need. A manager depends upon his staff services for accurate accounting, advertising skills, manufacturing control, sales strategy or many other functions. This kind of dependence is structured into any system where there is a division of labor. "What do you want me to do?" is a dependency question. In some settings it may be very appropriate. In other settings, this question may appear ridiculous, childish, or stupid. A child, seeking acceptance and affection, comes to mother again and again for assistance on the same problem. Finally,. the mother gets exasperated and says, "How many times must I do it for you?" A manager who continually manages by asking or getting his superiors to call the shots is the same problem in a business suit.

"Dependency is death." The grown person who makes dependent behavior the usual pattern literally gives up his or her right to their own uniqueness, inner power, and determination. They are other-directed, instead of inner-directed. Power is perceived as coming from others, not from self. Repetitive patterns of dependency in adults can increase the likelihood that a person will be incapable of coping with change or dealing with the life crises which come to everyone in the experience of multiple relationships: marriage, family, job, mobility, accidents, and death.

Dependency can be a very subtle affair. Most social institutions reinforce behavior patterns that perpetuate or draw people back into dependent relations. Not to decide is to decide. Very subtle. To belong we pay the price. Very obvious. Dependency is a continuous, lifelong struggle.

Dependency in work relationships is "Tell me what you want." This is very appropriate for starters in many situations. The dependent worker stops the initiated relationship at this point, playing it over and over, like a one-note polka. His invisible rules (norms) are "I'll do anything to please you. Just show me, please." His inner feelings have to do with his needs for acceptance, protection, and direction. Power is perceived as coming from other people, not from within the self. Dependent persons get their sense of worth by comparative evaluation with the source of their power and protection. Since the receiver is in the less powerful position in the relationship, this reinforces the image of self as not OK while the source is OK.

Dependency in work relations can be passive: "Don't make waves." Follow the rules. Go by the book. Say what the boss wants to hear. Aim only to please. Managers can aggressively pursue dependence: Be a super-pleaser. . .and get ahead. . .so long as there is someone above me to please, and who protects me. Again, a dependent manager can play it safe and bag his subordinates all at the same time by finding out what the boss wants and passing it on down as "God's word," thus remaining (in the subconscious fantasy) untouchable.

The big difference between dependence and interdependence lies in how the parties in a situation perceive and act on their power relationship. In a dependency situation one party acts in a way which says or implies, "I get my power from you. Tell me what you want. I want to please you." In an interdependent situation both parties act in a way which says or implies, "We both have inner power which we both respect. I can be me and you can be you. Let's use our power together."

THE STAGE OF COUNTERDEPENDENCE

Counterdependence begins when I question who I am, and begin to push outward to test myself and the world about me. Since I am questioning my own right to be OK, I must test myself against you, and all that is around me. Eric Fromm, commenting on the Eden theme, said, "That choice to assert self was the first step toward identity." The ability to push against, to question, and to test which this mode develops for a person is a needed and very functional skill when used appropriately by the adult. At its best, counterdependence is a process of pushing against, questioning, testing, searching, competing, and confirming of acceptable differentiations between self and others, a sorting out between this and that.

Along with the testing of self against others comes a basic change in power use (though the perception of it coming from outside self may not change). The counterdependent person resists power in others in order to find out how his own power is different from/better than others. He also uses his power on or over others. When a counterdependent person uses his power to push against, discover and affirm, it is a useful and needed process. Used to this end, counterdependence is a transitional or temporary mode.

In a developmental sense, counterdependence is ambivalent, going this way and that, fighting and hiding. The invisible rules (norms) are "Try and show me." "Don't do that some more." "I can do it all by myself." In the work setting, whatever you're for—I'll resist it—or at least have reservations. At the feeling level, counterdependence says, "I'll resist you, but I'm not sure I want to be totally responsible for my own actions. I like the shelter of dependency."

Counterdependence can become a life-style for people. The self-testing finds no resolution, and may be intensified by anxiety, aggression, or guilt. The I'm not OK feeling is still unmanaged.

And there may be a retreat back to dependency. Indeed, a counter-dependent person may be regularly riding a shuttle train back and forth between dependency and counterdependency. Such a person has not shifted his power perception to understand that his power does come from within. Thus the life-struggle does not move on; it only becomes more intense.

In the work setting, counterdependence as a life-style is very dysfunctional. Such persons are "jammers" who initiate blocking behavior. "Beat the system" is a common ploy. One-upmanship and overcompetitive behavior is usual. With peers, counterdependent persons usually compete at the wrong times and for the wrong purposes; i.e., over status rather than productive function, over coercive control rather than collaborative control. With subordinates, counterdependent persons become a do-for boss, a super-performer, a coercive or paternal overseer. With superiors, they are manipulators of the system. When they are on top they become paternal. Those on top who ride the shuttle train (see above) may tend to be coercive and punitive in one mode, and compliant and accommodating in the other.

The Win-Lose dynamic is a major power issue for counterdependent managers. Where people need to work together to get a job done, the person who needs to push against to prove something is bad news. The win-lose artist in such a setting generates unhelpful polarities and neutralizes energy by pitting force against force. Win-lose then leads to lose-lose.

For instance, when the fear of failure is so strong (not OK feelings about self) that a manager cannot own these feelings in himself or in the work situation, the net result is to multiply this fear in subordinates, thus trapping them into being energized by fear/dependency, resulting in only partial use of their resources. The winners then line up at the two-dollar window instead of the ten-dollar window. The difference was spent in resistance—like driving down the road with the pedal to the floor and the brakes on.

For instance, when a manager is a perfectionist (not OK feelings from being overcontrolled), the message to subordinates becomes "Enough is never enough." Subordinates feel distrust. It is hard to feel a sense of ownership in objectives. There is little motivation to set creative or ambitious goals. Dependency on the manager is reinforced, which in turn retraps the manager into "Enough is never enough." Win-lose all the way. A rebalancing of the internalized sense of power is the sought-for solution.

Managing conflict is a major issue for counterdependent managers. Elimination, coercion, avoidance, and denial are the usual win-lose options entertained. Win-win conditions, including discovery of the interdependent needs of conflicting parties, rehumanizing the other party, and resetting a power-on-power relationship for problem solving—all come hard and painfully. A creative work situation such as this involves people in the use and application of differences. This puts the counterdependent person at a disadvantage, because there may be lingering questions about his own OKness or about the OKness of others' differences and powers.

THE STAGE OF INDEPENDENCE

Independence is always a temporary position ("No man is an island. . . .He may think he's a whole continent, but. . . ."). It is an essential step in the journey from dependence to interdependence. To use the same metaphor as above, independence is when I take my voyage on the high seas of life. I affirm the reality of my own boundaries (the ship doesn't sink). I know there is power within me, that it is OK to assert myself as unique, to set my own counsel. I know my limitations. I respect the power in others and the world about me, although I don't understand and do question these things. My feeling about myself is that it's important for me to be on my own. Only I can be responsible for me. The invisible rules of independence were the buzz words of the 60s: "I'll do my thing. You do your thing."

In the work setting, independence is quite functional as a temporary style. The basic message is, "This is where it's at for me. Where are you?" Independence brings to the work setting clarity and assurance of boundedness, awareness of limitation and strength, a perspective on differences, and either a high personal motivation to task production or a distinctive air of measured indifference. The manager who uses independence with facility moves quickly to clarify and accept differentials in self and others, in power and resources. He easily declares the bounds of personal relationships. His natural tendency is to move toward interdependence.

As a habitual style, the independent manager may pose problems to his organization. His insularity may make him inaccessible to dependency-oriented subordinates. Others may not be able to use his resources in a situation where ambiguity and anxiety are high because he is perceived as inaccessible. In exercising initiative, he may slide back into the counterdependent mode of "I can do it all by myself" and satisfy himself in his heart of hearts that he is still independent, without realizing what has happened. In its worst aspects, this leads to "prima donna" behavior, which also moves back to counterdependence.

The biggest pitfall of the habitual independent is under-communication. As a corollary of this, he does not hold subordinates fully accountable. Within the circle of communication, he most often breaks the flow at the point of recommunicating what he hears and affirming or reaffirming the work of others.

All of this stems from the basic feeling stance of independence: "It's important for me to stand on my own. I know where I am, but I'm still not sure if I can accept others." Hence there are hesitation pitfalls. A habitual independent is particularly vulnerable to the hesitation pattern as a manager in high-pressure decisions involving people. The deep-down hesitation about acceptance of others (often not seen by the manager) causes prolongation of the decision. This behavior by senior managers results in people being "all torn up" at lower levels in the organization.

The long-term results of this kind of decision may further complicate life for the habitual independent. If the performance outcome of the people-decision is satisfactory, he will compliment himself on the decision and move on. If the performance outcome is superior or excellent, it may trigger questions of self-doubt, "Why did I hesitate?" or "Is this more than I bargained for?" If the performance outcome is less than satisfactory or not acceptable, it may reinforce the independent hesitation, or it could result in sliding back into a more defensive stance of counterdependence.

THE STAGE OF INTERDEPENDENCE

Moving to the interdependence level of human relations brings us to the affirmation of self and others in the developmental process. I'm OK. You're OK. In this mode, being OK is a matter of accepting that which is not OK along with that which is OK. In other words, the threshold of maturity is to be able to feel, "It's OK not to be all OK." Both of us accept and respect each other with our limitations. We know where we are and are capable of acting with internalized power. We both have power. I join my power with your power to generate or continue purposeful activity. We seek to build win-win power relationships. The feeling is, "I can be me, and you can be you." The invisible rules (norms) are "Let it be. . . ."mutual give-receive. Discovery is more satisfying or important than invention.

The interdependence of letting self and others be brings into our experience a new level of energy, new valuing, and new orientations toward work: the "sense of energy" in myself, which is so closely allied to my self-perception of power relationships with others, is now freed of its old goal. Yes, that energy is still in me. No, I don't have to expend it on proving myself. It's no longer a catch-up game. I am in a position to use my power not for filling deficiencies, but to be, to live "here-and-now." I can move beyond myself, be concerned about the restoration of the world so that life can continue, transcend the bounded world of trying to know and accept the reality that I can only be, I can never really know.

In work relationships the first message of interdependence is "I want from you. . . .What do you want from me?" Both parties initiate with power out of their own resources. Common needs, resources and objectives are explored. Negotiation and creative work styles are the patterns of interdependence. A sense of contract. . . .these are the ground rules. . . .this is what we'll do. . . .this is how we'll do it. . . .is the outcome. Thus contract building is one of the primary steps in building an interdependent management team.

The attitudes of interdependence are a helpful life-style for managers. Human organizations exist to do something for the environment, for the organization itself and for the people who make up the organization. Managers who are personally comfortable in mutual give-receive relationships can study the organization/environment interface, group interfaces, and the leadership/membership interface within the organization with candor. There is a commitment to sensing commonality and differential without getting hung up on personal deficiency needs or interpersonal conflict. When conflicts are sensed, they are sought out, clarified, and managed directly, rather than avoided.

THE IMPLICATIONS OF INTEREDEPENDENCE

Most authority relations in work *create dependency* as one of the initial factors in the situation. This is unavoidable. Differential in the structuring of accountability is necessary wherever there is division of labor. The key issue is *how* managers use the differential. Are authority and dependence used interdependently (power-with-power) or counterdependently (power-against-power)? Are competition and collaboration used at the right times for appropriate purposes?

For example, administrative or controllable expenses: one manager may be tough and coercieve on others below and around him initially, and then begin to manipulate the system for relief on this in the areas of his private interest. Another manager may recognize the underlying problem of consistency in broad-based commitment to control and thus work toward broadly negotiated commitments benefiting the whole organization, in which most parties have confidence and a commitment to make it happen.

A primary value for an interdependent manager is to preserve the OKness of all parties, so that the organization can devote maximum energy to goal achievement. He knows that the commitment of people to produce is directly related to their ability to influence the decisions that affect their work. He values the multiplier effect of win-win empowerment. His norm is: "I'll use my power in a way that helps you use your power." Thus he is concerned about the generation, distribution, and focusing of initiative and accountability throughout the system. From this perspective he sees three primary functions in his managerial role.

1) Sensing and managing the present issues on the major interfaces:
   Organization/environment
   Intergroup
   Leadership/membership
2) Sensing and planning for future issues on the major interfaces
3) Generating, distributing and focusing initiative and accountability

The interdependent manager uses all of the modes of power relations as they are appropriate. He is:

1) dependent when he needs information, resources, or skills not available in himself;
2) counterdependent when he needs to test, push against, confront, or explore;
3) independent when he needs self-expression. distance, or boundary clarification.

He tries to avoid:

1) dependence which seeks unnecessary direction, avoids responsibility, mirrors what others want, or destroys initiative;
2) counterdependence which is unneeded resistance, uses power on or over others needlessly, creates win-lose competition, excessively demanding, demeaning or punitive situations;
3) independence which creates unnecessary distance, over-differentiates boundaries, inappropriate self-expression, or blocks communication;
4) phony interdependence, where two parties lean on each other and disguise a double dependency as interdependence.

In setting accountabilities and building working contracts with groups and/or individuals, he looks carefully at the power relationships present or implied in the behavior of other managers:

1) Dependency:
   I must use yours.

2) Counterdependency:
   Yours is never any good.

3) Independence:
   I can use mine.

4) Interdependence:
   Let's use ours together.

GROWTH AND DEVELOPMENT

Persons who experience their power relations and self-perceptions through interdependence tend to move beyond the concern for personal power and adequacy. The spheres of concern on which personal energy is spent move outward. For our purposes here, we will look at three stages. The first stage is concern for human community. The second is for the generation and preservation of life and a world which will support life. The third is a concern for the experiencing of integrity and meaning in existence.

The first stage, concern for human community, is a mature social expression of our need for belonging. When I experience myself "letting be" and let others be also, authentic community is possible for the first time. Belonging to a community of valued persons takes on new importance. The importance of "here and now," the feelings of people rather than concerns over things, getting along with rather than getting ahead—all take on new values.

At this stage people like to manage and be managed in the participative way. Group problem solving and decision making become meaningful because life-energy is directed outward. There are inherent problems in group management. Managers working as a group may have one meeting after another and never get anything done. Individual accountability may be submerged or sidetracked for "groupness." The most basic internal problem in this impasse may be that not all the members of a group are really operating at this level, but are still focusing life-energy inward on personal adequacy. The most basic external reason for such an impasse is threat from the outside strong enough to throw the group into a survival mode.

It is at this point of participative malfunctions in group management that an organization faces one of its most crucial seductions and potentially disintegrative choices. It would appear that group management has "gone soft," or is overly concerned with membership issues and internal maintenance. At the task level, such problems may be a fact. The temptation is to regress to highly authoritarian or manipulative styles of management (both are counterdependent) and reassert dependency in subordinates.

The implications of this choice are that the organization, facing ineffective work, yields to the less-mature power tactics of dependency and counterdependency. The short-term effect is satisfying; the long-term effect is lose-lose. It settles for what appears to be a safer, surer solution of the task needs, using a fraction of the resources, rather than moving forward to deal with the task functions of the organization at interdependent levels, where more of the resource is usable. The effect of such a move on managers who are at the first level of interdependence may be to generate passive resistance of the worst order, and work effectiveness will go down.

A more effective alternative when group management "goes soft" is to move ahead to the second stage of interdependence where managers tend to apply their power to a balancing of productive effort and internal maintenance. This requires considerable assertion, modeling, and risk-taking on the part of the key manager.

At the second stage of interdependence the concern is for generation and preservation of life. At this point the value system of a person undergoes a major transformation. The depth and meaning of life multiply because I am spending my energy not on my life, but on life that is all about me. The common fears are manageable—fear of survival, fear of God, fear of the boss, fear of social disapproval. I want to spend my power on creative work that is valuable and has meaning beyond myself and my private world. My objective now is to use my power in a way that lets other people see, take, and use their power.

A manager living in this stage works hard and well. Overdirection turns him off. The task is to get the job done, not to get it done in a particular way. He is a good, creative goal setter because tasks that carry his efforts beyond himself turn him on. He values pluralism, because the world, all its things, all its people are important and interdependent. He values participative management because he senses life and pulse beyond the bodies in the group.

This is corporate life. His focus now is on facilitation and the best possible use of all the available human resources. A manager at this level is not easily blocked or diverted by task or process problems. He is confrontive in a spirit of support because he sees the necessity of keeping task and process work moving forward together. His sense of purpose and competence keep him moving straight to the point and he is highly effective in conflict management and problem solving.

At the third stage of interdependence a person focuses concern on integrity and the meaning of existence. In their own way, interdependent people find meaning in their work and also respect the meaning and integrity of other people's work. When a person moves to this level of experiencing, the realization comes that there is much he will never do, much he will never know about existence. This opens up two possibilities for enrichment of life to a manager.

The first possibility is transcendent—moving beyond present bounds. He may discover that a problem solving existence is not enough—the reality of existence is that you can only be. You can never really know or control with any sense of the ultimate. So he savors life from as wide a range of inputs as he can. There is renewed interest in cultural appreciation. Discovery becomes more important than invention. He is especially attuned to the relationship of the organization to its environment, its impact, value generation, and extended service to the wider community in various forms of public service.

The second possibility is internal. He may discover that he values those newer, deeply revealed moments in his own inner world which are there to be experienced. The richness is in listening, feeling, sharing. He values unity, simplicity, integrity. As a manager he focuses on the internal working and harmony of the organization. His emphasis is on doing human things. He may put considerable effort into bringing the contributions of others in the organization to full flower.

INTERDEPENDENCE IN GROUP MANAGEMENT

When organizations become complex, with many vertical lines of reporting relationships and many work group interfaces calling for lateral coordination, this greatly increases the need for inter-

dependent behavioral skills among managers. Multiple accountabilities, up, down, and lateral, are now required. A manager who is
used to relating vertically to one boss may play all sorts of games in
order to please and/or avoid the responsibility of being fully accountable and responsibly interdependent.

When the same manager is put into a matrix (criss-cross) system of multiple reporting relationships it introduces the polarity
issue: how to get along with *two* bosses? (It's like the child who
comes to the point of realizing he can no longer play off Mom and
Dad against each other. How does he learn to get along with both
parents?) The old assumptions about power relationships are upset.
More maturity in sharing power relationships is now a must. This
puts considerable stress on managers who formerly got by with so-so
relationships with bosses. The whole system is under stress at once,
because it is faced with the need to grow in the maturity of power
relationships.

Naturally the next question is, "How do we get from here to
there?" An interdependent system can be designed and implemented quickly. Developing an interdependent group of managers
with group behavior that will make it work well takes a while. One
of the major innovations in management science in this generation is
the use of behavioral scientists as third party process facilitators.
This approach helps management groups understand and improve
their on-job behavior so that they use their own and others'
resources more productively.

How does a management group develop its ability to work
interdependently?

First: It accepts designated leadership.

Second: It perceives a need to break the dependency between
         leader and members.

Third: There is commitment to use power accountably as
         individuals and collaboratively as a work group.

Fourth: Members own their own positions, confront and build
         a contract with the leader in which all parties are free
         to use their internalized sense of power and resource
         in:

   a. role relationships;

   b. ground rules for behavior;
   c. ability to manage differences;
   d. goals;
   e. work structure.

Fifth: The relationship is tested, expanded, revised with experience, with special focus on:

   a. new dependencies or counterdependencies;
   b. clear differentiation between personal power roles (working) and task authority roles (accountability);
   c. rechecking the ground rules;
   d. improving conflict management (creative use of differences).

The crucial issue is: *Can the designated leader and a work group break out of the structured dependency in their work relationship?* The initiative to do this must come from within the work group. However, the real stress in breaking leader dependency lies on the leader himself, not on the subordinates. The subordinates do feel stress, coercion, frustration. They do sense risk in confronting authority, and will initiate the confrontation if the risk is not too great. But the leader for whom this differential of authority and responsibility is very real has an even greater risk. How does he exercise his authority in a way which achieves the tasks for which he is responsible, and at the same time does not trap his subordinates in dependency? Differentiation in levels of authority and responsibility *creates* dependency. Whether or not leader and subordinates *act* dependently or otherwise is a matter of behavior. The behavior depends on how a person feels about himself and how he sees his own power.

The leader's dilemma is the need to maintain functional levels of task authority in a chain of command (superior-subordinate) while at the same time maintaining a balanced, personal power dynamic (interdependence) among those with whom he works. The structured superior-subordinate authority relationship of the task organization tends to trap persons into behaving in the dependency relationship of the child, where one person is powerless and depends on another for power. In the one-to-group relationship this sets a coercive norm: only one person can exercise power. The desired norm is collaboration: all can exercise power.

The leader is caught up in a dilemma not unlike the father-son dilemma: the father wants very much to affirm his son's manhood. But he cannot give his son his manhood. The son can only take it for himself. Once the son takes his manhood, the father can affirm it. Any effort by the father to affirm what the son will not take for himself is a block (or castration) to the son. In reverse, if the son claims the manhood (responsibility, authority) which he wants without fulfilling the obligations, the son not only debases himself, but the father as well. The limitation and risk for the father are very real.

The manager's dilemma is real: He has responsibility and authority (a form of power). If he delegates some of this to subordinates, and they continue to act dependently on him, he has lost some of his power. Delegation can mean loss. Is it worth the risk? Is it retrievable? At what cost to himself, to the subordinates? The manager has good reason to manage counterdependently, reserving power to himself, until he has some assurance that sharing the power will not diminish his own power to be effective. He has good reason to question participative sharing until he has a sense that, once shared, it will not be abdicated and lost, to the detriment of one, the other, or both parties. Hence, until the power dynamics of personal interdependence are perceived, expressed, and tested, he has good reason to be cautious about taking risks in sharing and delegation which may result in irretrievable loss of power and control in a task situation.

This puts an additional stress on the leader. *The most important factor in whether a work group can break out of the dependency trap is how the leader perceives and handles his own feelings of dependency, counterdependency, independence, and interdependence.* The leader's own behavior sets the stage, determines the dimensions of the dependency problem with which the group must cope. (An additional consideration: the norms or invisible rules which the overarching culture of the organization set upon a leader also help determine the dimensions of the dependency issue.)

In working toward interdependence with a work group, the leader continues to use his power fully in ways which make it possible for others to take up and use their power. He asks for and follows through on high responsibility, accountability, and initiative from his subordinates.

Learning to break out of leader dependency is one of the hardest moves any manager makes in his career. It appears that a high percentage never do. Some do, but return to it. And those who do break out, perceive that they must break out again and again.

SUMMARY

Four Power Styles

	Dependence	Counterdependence	Independence	Interdependence
Work	Tell me what you want. Do this for me.	Whatever you're for. . .I'll resist it – or at least have reservations. That's not enough.	This is where it's at for me. . . Where are you?	I want from you. . . . What do you want from me?
	(Follow)	(Test)	(Assert)	(Join)
Norms	I'll do anything to please you. Show me, please.	Try and show me. Don't do that some more. Enough is never enough. I can do it all by myself.	I'll do my thing. You do your thing.	Let it be. . . .Mutual give-receive. Discovery is° more important than invention.
Attitudes	Please accept me, feed me, take care of me. You *must* take care of me.	I'll resist you, but I'm not sure I want to be responsible for my own actions. I still like the shelter of dependency.	It's important for me to stand on my own. Only I can be responsible for my actions.	I can be me, and you can be you. Our differences are important.
Power	I get power from you.	I resist power in others to find how my power is different from (better than) others.	I use my power to assert my uniqueness.	We both have power. I join my power with your power to do things that matter.
Uses	Utilizing external or different resources.	Testing reality, workability. Extending self, influence, boundary, power.	Exercising initiative. Maintaining boundaries or autonomy.	Collaboration in work. Appreciation and valuing.
Misuses	Not using own power. Playing it safe, coasting, free-loading.	Blocking, inhibiting, fighting, or withholding which cancels out other's efforts.	Isolated, disruptive unilateral actions. Undercommunicating. Ignoring accountability.	Hidden dependency. "Masking." Leaning on other people.
Relations	You win - I win You lose - I lose I'm Not OK You're OK	You win - I lose You lose - I win I'm OK? You're OK?	I win Indifference I'm OK You're OK?	I win - you win You win - I win I'm OK You're OK

WHAT REALLY COUNTS FOR ME?

Personal goals are vital for the organizational success of MBO/R. In our earlier book we used a model that included Hughes's presentation of the necessary interaction between individual and organization goals as part of the goal setting process.[1] These personal goals need to include not only those items directly related to work, but also those that are significant for the individuals in their nonwork activities. This places much greater demands on the individual, as well as management, relative to handling the goal setting process.

THE IMPORTANCE OF THE PERSONAL ASPECT

In a section titled "The Manager's Secret Personal Goals," Humble seems to have identified the reality of the issue: "Some feel that these are personal questions that have nothing to do with business. But that is a serious delusion, and any MBO system that does not concern itself with the answers to these questions will be heading toward failure."[2] It is this type of situation that emphasizes the need for an organization to be able to work its values issue in a way that supports or denies the emPOWERment approach. If the organization's values and norms do not accept the reality of the total human resource, there will be no place for these concerns in the management process—and Humble's conclusion will very likely occur. With acceptance, however, comes the need to answer the question: What really counts for me?

Dealing with this question will usually require an organizational commitment to a personal growth concept that goes far beyond a manager's suggesting that a subordinate read a book or go to a seminar to get "shaped up." Our experience has been that relatively few individuals are in a position to do much more than conform to what they think the boss or the organization wants. There is a need for the organization implementing MBO/R to provide a variety of learning experiences and growth opportunities to facilitate personal development in balance with career development. These would help individuals to become more aware of themselves, their skills and competencies, and supportively build their self-concept by working with techniques such as values clarification, Transactional Analysis, and life or career planning. This type of development is very helpful for the emPOWERment process. These techniques also have a high potential for facilitating positive coping with the personal dilemmas that many individuals are experiencing relative to midcareer obsolescence or "doldrums."

LIFE PLANNING AS A BASIS FOR PERSONAL GOALS

Life planning is a micro-MBO process that helps individuals—or couples—identify their personal goals; inventory their skills, strengths, and weaknesses; establish time lines; and clarify who (or what) is controlling their lives.[3] This activity is sometimes referred to as career planning. Its purpose is to identify what it is that *you* want and to develop action plans for achieving that RESULT.

Life planning needs to deal with the "whole" person on an around-the-clock basis. Though some organizations and MBO writers have supported writing personal goals relative to the work environment, our approach includes both on- and off-the-job aspects of life. In an open climate, this has high potential for maximizing the effective utilization of the people in the organization. Having clarity about your personal goals and resources facilitates the management of differences in the emPOWERment process. It also contributes to a strong self-concept, personal motivation, and a new sense of personal freedom by having clarified the boundaries of your life style.

To engage in this process, however, one must be willing to accept a significant level of responsibility and accountability for oneself. Current organization experience is not too supportive of such a position because the typical situation is more likely to be oriented toward maintaining dependency. Thus, coming to know more of the reality of your own power can produce a level of fear that may cause individuals to defensively resist the change and growth process. Unless the organization is truly supportive throughout, individuals are likely to experience a serious "double-bind." But most individuals seem to be willing to risk while opening up their potential in order to realize the growth that they sense is available through the process if the organization is concurrently supportive with openness and trust building.

The life planning process or workshop may deal with a variety of very personal issues such as values, work, career, life-style, and life scripts (from Transactional Analysis). These are examined in various ways to develop awareness about:

Who am I?

Where am I in my life?

What do I want in my life?

What RESULTS do I want based on the foregoing data?

Developing answers to these questions is a micro-MBO process in that we are using essentially the same total process but scaling it down for application at the individual level. The elements of the process are:

- Data collection   developing information about yourself.
- Forecasting   creating the future that you desire for yourself.
- Focusing   identifying some areas in which you really want to make some things happen.
- Goal setting   establishing some end RESULTS that you want to achieve.
- Action planning   writing short-term objectives and making action plans for achieving them.

- Implementing   carrying out the plans to produce RESULTS.

- Review and   comparing achievements to the desired
  evaluation   outcomes in order to take corrective future actions.

There are an increasing number of workshop designs available to facilitate the development of the information and self-understanding needed to work through the life planning process.[4] This process is most frequently used in a group setting, but is equally appropriate for individual or one-to-one counseling. The group provides comfort and support in the sharing activities and is a rich resource for new ideas and different possibilities for solving problems.

APPLICATION IN THE GOAL SETTING PROCESS

When individuals have worked through their life-planning cycle to the point where they are into the implementation aspect of it, they are in a much stronger position relative to the organization. As mentioned previously, it is a very positive situation when the organization's values are supportive of personal growth and collaborative (participative) goal setting and management. When the value system or climate is not supportive, individuals need to be cautious with their "new" power. Individuals with this direction and force in their lives can be very threatening to a boss, peer, or subordinate who is still functioning in a highly dependent manner. Therefore, it is wise to integrate this new energy with understanding so as to avoid an abrasive change in the existing organizational balance point.

With either condition the most practical approach to handling the change seems to be through negotiating "psychological" contracts for role clarity within the organization. This is described more completely in Chapter 9 but, basically, it means that individuals develop agreements relative to the nature of their work functions and relationships. This is a matching of the expectations of each other on a variety of issues. Constructively and creatively we are seeking to balance the individual and organization concerns relative to how we will work together. This tends to provide more freedom for individuals to perform and contribute to organization RESULTS since they are aware of the expectations and can put their energy into work accomplishment rather than into "self-protection" due to various levels or types of fear.

Personal growth and life planning are major issues in the area of personal development. Due to the psychological and behavioral implications they will have a marked effect on the implementation and success of Management by Objectives for RESULTS. Truly, this is where management skills have a high impact. Managers, and subordinates, must be able to cope with and be accountable for the responses to these questions:[5]

- What are you going to do for the organization this year?
- What are you going to do for yourself this year?
- How can we help?

Life planning, as part of a fully functioning MBO/R program, will provide the basis for an in-depth response that will maximize personal effectiveness as part of achieving organization RESULTS.

NOTES

1. A.C. Beck, Jr. and E. D. Hillmar 1972. *A practical approach to organization development through MBO—selected readings.* Reading, Mass.: Addison-Wesley, Preface.

2. J.W. Humble 1973. *How to manage by objectives.* New York: AMACOM, pp. 5-6.

3. Adapted from R.N. Bolles 1973. *What color is your parachute?* Berkeley, Calif.: Ten Speed Press, p. 70.

4. The following is a representative listing of sources for workshop designs: Bolles, R.N. 1973. *What color is your parachute?* Berkeley, Calif.: Ten Speed Press, pp. 59-104.

   Ford, G. A., and G. L. Lippitt 1972. *A life planning workbook.* Fairfax, Virginia: NTL Learning Resources Corporation.

   Kay, J.A. 1973. In D. Jongeward, and D. Scott (eds.). What do I want to do next? *Affirmative Action for Women.* Reading, Mass.: Addison-Wesley, pp. 251-286.

   Kirn, A., and M. Kirn 1974. Life/work planning. *The 1974 Annual*

Handbook for Group Facilitators. La Jolla, Calif.: University Associates Publishers, pp. 189–195.

Lippit, G. 1970. Developing life plans. *Training and Development Journal* (May), pp.2–7.

Pfeiffer, J.W. and J.E. Jones (eds.) 1970. *A handbook of structured experiences for human relations training, Vol. II.* Iowa City: University Associates Press, pp. 113–127.

5. W. Bull 1973. Compensation managers: let's not sleepwalk the 70s. *Canadian Business Quarterly* (Winter): p. 25.

WHAT DO YOU MEAN I'M NOT GETTING RESULTS?

The title of this chapter is a quote from a rather indignant partici-
pant in an MBO/R workshop. It had just been suggested to him
that the work activity he had described did not have the RESULTS
orientation that must be developed for MBO/R to be most effective.
He had described a work/job activity which kept him very busy and
was important, but his attention was focused on the "means," not
the "end."

One of the significant barriers to be overcome in making
MBO/R work is the dilemma: "Is this a RESULT or an activity?"
This is a critical issue since we must identify the RESULTS we seek
at all levels throughout this total process. However, when the issue is
not clearly understood and the emphasis is placed on writing objectives, the normal tendency is to generate an activity orientation
rather than a RESULTS orientation.

UNDERSTANDING WHAT RESULTS ARE

Drucker has described RESULTS as " contributions to the market
or achievement toward goal and objectives . . . ."[1] The difficulty in
practice seems to lie in understanding how that relatively simple
statement translates into working application. Here, again, Drucker
has provided a basis for clarification:

> Business performance therefore requires that each job be
> directed toward the objectives of the whole business. And in

particular each manager's job must be focused on the success of the whole. The performance that is expected of the manager must be derived from the performance goals of the business, his results must be measured by the contribution they make to the success of the enterprise. The manager must know and understand what the business goals demand of him in terms of performance, and his superior must know what contribution to demand and expect of him—and must judge him accordingly.[2]

The key to understanding and application is inherent in having the focus on the contribution and performance of the whole organization. This requires *organizational* goal statements that clearly identify the expected "end" condition (RESULTS), not the "means" (activities) to achieving it. In Chapter 1 reference was made to Howell's three stages of MBO. Most organizations seem to have made Stage I applications which are primarily "individual" in their emphasis. Consequently, little has been done to clearly identify organization RESULTS or "contributions to the market."

We believe that our MBO/R process is a Stage II approach which means that management must clearly state the organization's purpose and goals as well as manage the integration of individual performance for the realization of those goals while moving toward the purpose or mission. For most organizations this represents a significant change in management style and will require work with OD and planning methodology.

Group process skills as described in later chapters are particularly helpful in working to identify organization RESULTS. In our workshops, individuals have often indicated that they were told what their objectives would be, but that they had no direct knowledge of their boss's objectives nor of any organizational objectives. In working with the MBO/R process you soon begin to seek clear organization RESULTS so that you can direct your individual achievement toward that end. As you begin to work organizational issues there will be more situations where various groups and subgroups will need to come together to solve problems, make decisions, or coordinate various aspects of the job.

Developing RESULTS statements means that we have to express our performance in terms of the condition that it will create outside of our own group or system rather than describing our own internal job activities. The final test of your individual or organizational achievement is made in terms of what difference it has made for someone else. This is the essence of being able to separate activities from RESULTS.

With the predominant emphasis on individuals and what they are doing, we have been conditioned to think in terms of accomplishing the job (work) functions and not RESULTS. The underlying assumption seems to be: If you work hard enough, you *should* produce RESULTS. Thus, the concern is on activities or the "How" aspect. The MBO/R approach starts with the desired RESULTS—"What"—then we plan and manage the work effort that will be necessary to achieve it.

The activity orientation often limits individuals and creates a dependency condition in which persons rely heavily on a job description or management to tell them what to do. Working from the RESULTS orientation is, however, emPOWERing. It provides a more creative situation in which there is considerable freedom for personal growth and development. The differences are subtle. Yet, they can create significantly different behavior and achievement within the organization. In later chapters there will be others but some typical illustrations of the difference in focus between activities and RESULTS are:

taking X-rays	versus	informed diagnosis
making movies	versus	entertainment of people
processing data	versus	decisions made
making light bulbs	versus	illumination systems
selling insurance	versus	protection and security

AN ESSENTIAL MBO/R SKILL

The ability to think and conceptualize in terms of RESULTS is an essential skill for making MBO/R work. Though top management is frequently able to respond with this focus, there is a need for it to be prevalent throughout the organization if we are to maximize the use of our human resources. Typically, the RESULTS identified by upper management have been quickly translated into directed activities which are then passed down through the organization as "orders (goals) from above."

In order to develop this skill of conceptualizing in terms of RESULTS, individuals and organizations must think beyond their own boundaries. It means we must be secure in our own identity so that we are free enough to be aware of the demands that others are making of us or our work group. The key here is that rather than looking within to improve our own efficiency we must, first, look outside to validate that our RESULTS are meeting the needs and values of the total environment in which we are functioning. This approach runs counter to most of our historical experience that is based on a rational, mechanistic philosophy which says you should first seek to get your own work perfect and that should give you the "best" performance. But if you don't know what the "market" needs, what good is it to become superefficient at doing something that might not be needed or which is of marginal value in terms of organizational performance and achievement.

Another aspect of developing this skill is to maintain a high level of awareness as to where your concern is focused. In order to cope with the almost instantaneous changes from your own individual concern to organizational concerns, you must be able to differentiate between what is central—figure—and what is the surrounding in which that is happening—(back)ground. Many of you will have experienced the psychological experiment in which you look at a picture which you may see as a light vase or two opposing silhouetted profiles. This is a matter of perception and being aware of which of those is the "figure" at any instant. This same type of perception or awareness is needed to be able to work with the conceptual changes in moving from individual to organizational concerns, from input to output and from activities to RESULTS.

THE REASON BEHIND IT ALL: ACCOUNTABILITY

Many have asked: "Why go to all this extra work? Why bother with all of this? I'm getting my job done. Is it worth the effort?" We think that the answers lie in each organization's value system relative to accountability. There is, certainly, a high potential for increased productivity with MBO/R, but that is somewhat relative in terms of being accountable for an agreed upon level of productivity.

Unless an individual/organization is accountable, there is little justification for seeking a RESULTS orientation. If there is no real commitment to working the accountability issue, there is little justification for engaging in the MBO/R process. The true payoff will be lost without the discipline of managing the accountability for RESULTS. This accountability needs to be directed not only towards work or task achievement, but also towards maintaining relationships and affirming one's self.

We are all under increasing pressure for effectiveness in achieving RESULTS—organization RESULTS in our view. This approach includes considerable emphasis on shared or joint responsibility and accountability for contributing to and achieving those RESULTS. In itself this is somewhat of a step forward compared to past management practice. But this change is part of the necessary movement forward. If we are to have motivating achievement at the individual and organizational level and provide rewards based on real performance rather than personality or influence, there must be a solid basis for being accountable. Accountability based on contribution to organization RESULTS leads to managing for the effective utilization of *all* the resources available.

The readings included with this chapter provide illustrations of how putting the focus on RESULTS changes the organizational behavior pattern as it moves away from activities (Schleh: "Grabbing Profits by the Roots") and the challenge for managers to demand and get improved performance (Schaffer: "Demand Better Results—and Get Them").

NOTES

1. P.R. Drucker 1974. *Management.* New York: Harper & Row, p. 142.
2. _____ 1954. *Practice of management.* New York: Harper & Row, p. 121.

GRABBING PROFITS BY THE ROOTS: A CASE STUDY IN "RESULTS MANAGEMENT"

EDWARD C. SCHLEH

It is the job of an executive to maximize the return from the assets and talents of his organization. This task is made doubly difficult in an inflationary period by the cost-price whirl. It is particularly difficult in a large, far-flung organization; the limbs of the elephant do not react as quickly as do those of the mouse.

Executives must turn to intensified mining of the latent abilities of all members of the organization. This means new approaches to management.

This report is a case study of how the application of a ."results-management" approach to a large profit center increased its profit contribution 35 percent in three years.

What is results management?

An organization is extremely fortunate if it capitalizes on as much as 50 percent of the talent of its key management people. A person in a management position is subjected to pressures—both positive and negative—caused by delegation, accountability systems, budget systems, policy, corporate relationships, and so on. *Results management is a series of principles that act as a kind of catalyst to reduce the negative pressures and increase the positive ones so that the firm can increase the return from the large reservoir of ability that lies dormant in its management people.*

The profit center to be described is a region of the American Oil Company, the domestic refining and marketing subsidiary of Standard Oil Company (Indiana) and the fourth-ranking petroleum marketer in the country. (American held this position in 1970 with only 7.3 percent of the national gasoline market. At that time, it ranked less than 1 percent behind the leader, thus indicating the intensity of competition in this business.)

This region covers 13 states. Its total sales of refined products exceed two billion gallons per year, with most of this volume distributed and sold through independent dealers and jobbers, who are not company employees. The region already was recognized as an effective marketing organization, and the effort described here was an attempt to apply a sophisticated management approach in order to further improve its profit contribution.

The line organization of the region consisted of marketing representatives, field sales managers, district managers, and the regional vice-president. Six major staff groups were set up to service this line—marketing, distribution, administrative, pricing, planning, and employee relations.

An essential in a results approach is to clarify the overall purpose of the organization and, from this, the focus of management operation.

It became clear that a primary focal point of the marketing department—the reason for the existence of the region—*should be service to the motorist.* Essentially, the *motorist had to be looked on as the customer.* This meant that a realistic approach was to look at the dealers as the bottom of the marketing chain, even though they were independent operators.

Previously, the region had been operating as if the dealer were the customer. This was natural, because the dealer actually ordered products from American and paid for them. He was sold products on the assumption that if he built up inventories, this would result in increased sales to the motorist. Less attention was given to training the dealer how to merchandise products and, particularly, how to teach his attendants to give better service to the customer.

Redirecting the marketing department's focus to the motorist led quite logically to a change in thinking about the job of a marketing representative. The job's main thrust was changed from trying to sell the dealer products for inventory to helping him merchandise products and making him successful.

To do this, the marketing representative had to be capable of teaching dealers and their station attendants how to give service and sell products. It was clear that more intensified instruction on how to train would be advantageous, so a training program was set up for this purpose, still recognizing that the dealer was independent.

A key principle of results management is that good supervision always pays off in terms of the results you want. The most important place for good supervision is not at the top, as is commonly supposed, but at the first level.

The region had been well set up so that the complement under each of the first-level field sales managers was small enough to be manageable. Each had five marketing representatives reporting to him. The problem was that the field sales manager was operating primarily as a senior salesman. In effect, he was downgrading supervision.

The job of the field sales manager, therefore, was changed so that its prime emphasis would be on developing marketing representatives so that they could make the dealers more successful. As a first step, the field sales managers were trained more intensively how to teach their marketing representatives to train dealers and attendants. With strong first-level supervision, the number of managers to be supervised can be increased. In this case, three districts were eventually eliminated and consolidated into others, because more responsibility was being assumed by the field sales managers.

Because marketing representatives would naturally follow the direction indicated by their managers—the field sales managers—and they, in turn, followed the direction indicated by the district managers, the role of the district manager was the next point of study.

The district manager primarily had been accountable for volume, because major emphasis had been placed on carrying out merchandising programs developed by the central office. On the surface, the emphasis on merchandising programs shouldn't have caused any problems, because most of these programs were supposed to be voluntary. In other words, the district had the option of using or not using these programs, as it saw fit, depending on the circumstances in the district.

In practice, however, rankings were made up to show which of the districts did well and which ones did poorly on a particular program. Obviously, no district manager would want to be on the lower end of such rankings. In practice, therefore, all the programs were compulsory, thus causing an imbalance. For example, many minor profit items were given as much—and sometimes more—emphasis as were major profit items. In addition, the dealer's success and servicing of the motorist were not highlighted.

ACCOUNTABILITY BASED ON PROFIT CONTRIBUTION

Results management is geared toward balancing the emphasis on all the results expected of a manager in order to minimize slippage.

To encourage such a situation, district managers were placed on an accountability system based on profit contribution. A true profit-and-loss statement for a district was almost impossible to prepare in light of all the accounting allocation complexities that were involved; however, such a statement was not necessary. The idea was to encourage the district manager to act in the best direction of profit contribution. For this purpose, only data on general allocations of controllable costs were needed.

An economic performance index was developed that excluded overhead and headquarters costs, terminal costs, refinery charges, and taxes and that was aimed at those items most affected by the district managers. The goal of the economic performance index was to encourage a district manager to take a realistic view of that volume that did not contribute well to profit when compared with the energy required.

As a case in point, after the economic performance index was set up, one district manager made an unprecedented recommendation that nine million gallons of gasoline sales be turned down because he could better use the time getting more profitable volume.

The economic performance index also was essential if the district manager were to be given more authority to control his district's problems. A fundamental principle of results management is that *authority should never be given without accountability. Otherwise, it is difficult to control the direction in which decisions are made. Also, it is generally best to push authority to the lowest level possible.* This economic performance index made it possible to delegate more authority to the district managers.

For example, the repair and maintenance of service stations for all districts previously had been supervised by the distribution department in the regional office. This function was now broken up and a foreman of maintenance put under each district manager.

Maintenance's function was to maintain stations and equipment so that they would be more effective in serving motorists.

Because district managers were now accountable for the cost of this maintenance, they could more quickly decide where to place their maintenance money. This eliminated a considerable amount of red tape. District managers also were less inclined to "gold plate" certain stations now that the maintenance budget was their own.

They became quite careful of their maintenance dollars because they were accountable for both the value received from maintenance and its cost. This follows the results principle that *the accountability system should encourage a manager to emphasize all the important results that are expected of him.*

JOINT ACCOUNTABILITY

Obviously, some help from staff was necessary to train these maintenance foremen and feed them new ideas, because the district manager would not be an expert on maintenance. Therefore, the area engineers of the distribution department were given the responsibility of training these maintenance people and were held accountable for total maintenance effectiveness in their areas, even though they were staff. This was possible under the joint-accountability principle of results management. Under this principle, *two people may be held accountable for the same result if both have a major contribution to make to it.*

Part of the profit problem of a district involved credit. Formerly the credit function had been centralized in a regional credit department, which took its loss prevention role quite seriously. Decisions took time, and considerable correspondence with the marketing representatives was required.

Because the district manager was now accountable for profit in his district, the credit responsibility was shifted to him and to the field sales managers under him. They, in turn, delegated this responsibility to the marketing representatives. This move pushed the action to the lowest line-level possible—an aim of results management.

This setup could not have worked well if the central credit people had not been given the responsibility of training the district personnel in credit management. Under results management, *a prime job of a central staff is to train the line management in the area of the staff's expertise, not to do all the work itself.*

For the system to be effective, the central staff had to be accountable, along with the district personnel, for credit losses and for the effect of credit on sales—another illustration of joint accountability in practice. Under the new setup, a number of credit representatives were no longer needed, and as the marketing representatives were trained, better credit decisions could be made closer to the dealer.

COST IMPACT ON THE LINE

Another problem that became apparent involved the percentage of the marketing representative's time that was not spent on helping to make the dealer successful. From a results-management point of view, *the purpose of all staff is to help the line people to be more effective.* This is almost the reverse of the way that the staff had been operating.

The marketing representatives had been looked at as aides who carried out the staff's programs—as many as 28 of these programs simultaneously. A belief had developed that the marketing representative could do many things in the district for staff because he was "going there anyway," forgetting that the cost of a man on the road was anywhere from $10 to $15 an hour.

As a result, there were many requests from staff for surveys, reports, and other special studies. Staff also required many follow-up letters on problems. In addition, the requests for reports often had such short time fuses on them that the marketing representative had to drop everything to meet the deadline.

To increase the time that the marketing representative could spend on his basic job—that is, making the dealer successful—each of the people requesting help was required to estimate the time involved in the request, its costs, and the value expected, with the estimate approved by the region. For example, if the time required for a request was one day per marketing representative, and 100 marketing representatives at $100 per day were involved, the request would cost $10,000. It was then up to the staff man to show where a profit could be obtained from this expenditure.

Thus, *staff was made accountable for its costs impact on the line.* This led to a reduction in the number of some requests and to more economical substitutes for others.

The accountability system acts as a strong pressure on any person in a job. Program accountability, for example, had resulted in short-term emphasis on special product sales that had frequently been bolstered by special program rewards that were tied to a particular program. These programs, though, did not apply to every territory, because seasonal differences often existed, and the same product could not be pushed in several territories at the same time.

In addition, with program pushes, marketing representatives were encouraged to save up sales for a particular program. As a consequence, year-round selling was often discouraged.

To prevent these problems, the accountability system was changed. The goals of marketing representatives, field sales managers, and district sales managers were set on a yearly basis, and appraisals were changed to reflect this. Corresponding changes were made in programs. For example, special incentive programs were scheduled for a whole year instead of a short time.

MANAGING BY OBJECTIVES

In results management *the objectives for each job should be based on the problems of that job in a particular period.* This is the best way to direct a manager to contribute to company results. Every territory, field area, or district may have objectives that differ from its counterparts, because its current problems are different.

One of the primary problems with firms' setting management objectives is that they tend to set uniform objectives for all similar jobs. This is almost invariably an inappropriate approach for getting maximum results from the jobs and, in many cases, leads to imbalance.

Before objectives were set, therefore, each management person went through job-purpose training.

This is a step-by-step process in which a person clarifies with his manager what the company results are that his job should be aiming at in a particular period. The prime questions that are explored are: Where can I best contribute to the company in this period? What would be lost if I weren't here? What impact do I have on results that are expected of other jobs? Through this process, people learn to think more deeply about their potential impact on company results.

The process is more effective if there is no attempt to measure objectives at the time. When firms jump to objectives without going through this step, they often set objectives that actually misdirect the employee.

The regional marketing staff then was analyzed from the same results standpoint. In results management, *staff should always aim at line results.* In other words, it is staff's function to help line to do its job better.

In the past, the regional marketing staff had looked at its job as partly transmitter of home office programs and partly supervisor of these programs in the field. This thinking had grown from the idea that the staff was an extension of the executive. As a consequence, staff was often adding to the emphasis on low-profit products. For example, gasoline made up 80 percent of the profit but accounted for only 10 percent of the programs. Many staff merchandise men had been set up in the home office, with responsibility for different programs, and each wanted to make a showing with his program.

Each program seemed perfectly logical, looking at it from a national point of view. However, each staff man takes the time of line people to do his work. Many communications, therefore, were required from staff to the field and back again.

MAKING DEALERS SUCCESSFUL

As part of the change in orientation, the regional staff was also conditioned to think in terms of making the dealers more successful. One important way was the development of merchandising and training methods with which the district personnel would train the dealer and his attendants.

To start with, the regional staff was taught how to work training methods into all the programs that they passed on to the districts. With dealer effectiveness as the target, it was also possible to weed out those merchandising programs that did not fit the region.

The region had previously recognized the problem of building up dealers' effectiveness in merchandising. At that time, three field merchandisers had been set up to work in a station with just a few dealers, training attendants and dealers to handle customers and merchandise better. This solution was a partial application of

Frederick Taylor's specialization approach to parts of supervision and had been very successful. However, the dealers started to look to these merchandisers rather than to the marketing representatives for solutions to almost every problem. In effect, the marketing representative was being cut out; he was not accountable for the total result, and his relationship with the dealer was weakened.

The ideas and techniques developed by these field merchandisers were excellent, but only a limited number of dealers were covered. With a little different approach, these field merchandisers' knowledge was used to cover more dealers. This was done by having the merchandisers train the field sales managers and representatives in merchandising and other methods.

Better line accountability results if training methods are handled through the manager—in this case, the field sales manager. Supervision also is strengthened. To get the job done quickly, however, the merchandisers went out and personally coached the marketing representatives on how to train dealers and dealer assistants to carry out certain merchandising methods and to analyze their profitability. They also advised the representatives on how to best utilize their own time.

Some marketing representatives who were used to the old program method started dealer-training clinics and considered their job to be that of simply running these training clinics. These representatives had to be conditioned to think in terms of accountability for dealer results rather than the number of clinics held. The number of clinics held is merely an activity; their purpose, if properly run, should be to make the dealer more effective.

With the new field-merchandiser setup, several regional merchandise managers who had been working on programs were unnecessary and could be eliminated. Also, with the new merchandising setup in the line, the advertising manager in the regional office was no longer necessary. Advertising usually came from the home office, and whatever additional help was necessary in the region could be handled by the reseller manager, who was the regional overall marketing staff man.

The school for dealers also was changed so that it included training in how to teach attendants and additional instruction in mechandising and business management.

IMPACT OF FINAL RESULTS

The remaining regional staff was then analyzed from the point of view of its impact on final results at the dealer level. A major area studied was that involving planning capital installations.

In the main, the company owned the stations and leased them to independent dealers. The work was organized by function: new business representatives went out to find locations and to tie up the real estate; engineering did all the planning and controlling of construction; legal handled its aspects; and economic analysis and evaluation personnel evaluated profit potential of prospective locations. The tie-in among these people had been loose; each had gone his own independent way. Installations, therefore, were often late, and the planning didn't fully respond to the needs of the field.

To eliminate this situation, the role of the planning department was broadened so that all the functions that were necessary for a capital installation were put under this department. The head of the department then could be accountable for a total result—on-stream stations within specified time and cost goals and producing the profits expected.

Organization generally gets better results if a manager can be made accountable for total results and, in addition, can be given control of all those items that lead to these results.

This rule was applied more thoroughly. Project managers were set up in charge of capital installations for sections of the region, and the various specialists needed for projects in that section were assigned to them. This setup built in tight accountability with a quick-acting, small group. The effect of this move was to cut the staff considerably, because less time was required for coordination. What was more important, the time needed to get new stations on-stream was reduced considerably.

LONG-RANGE VERSUS SHORT-RANGE PLANNING

In analyzing the planning department, it became clear that long-range planning had been somewhat shortchanged. It is a results-management rule that *long-range results should be separated from short-range results.* The crisis—in this case, the yearly station building program—always looms large. A special planning manager, therefore, was set up to handle long-range planning of installations. He worked out a number of successful methods for handling special leasing in certain areas and getting new stations on-stream and an entirely new scheme for combining various subsidiary companies more fully into the American Oil Company. The latter substaintially improved company profit in heating oils by eliminating duplications and redirecting efforts.

As a result of removing service-station engineering and maintenance from the distribution department and placing them in the planning department and in the district, the remainder of the distribution department was primarily a service to the reseller sales operation—the group that sold through dealers. The head of the distribution department, therefore, was placed directly under the marketing manager, thus tying the department more firmly to the result that it served.

After the transfers out of maintenance and engineering for service-station construction, a distribution manager of the combined engineering, maintenance, and terminal sections was no longer necessary, so that job was eliminated. Within the department, two highly skilled distribution men had operated as staff specialists for the 38 terminals of the department; however, they were not fully accountable for any of the terminals. According to results management, *staff service is rarely a substitute for line.* In this case, these staff jobs were eliminated and the men reassigned to two new line jobs as managers of field distribution. Each was given half of the terminals to supervise directly and was made accountable for results in those terminals, for their service to the marketing group, and for their cost.

COST PICTURE

Under the new setup, costs were considerably reduced in the terminals by the work of the field distribution managers. Stock loses showed a dramatic reduction, especially because the district manager, who was now working on a profit basis, was quite interested in cooperating with the distribution department in reducing these losses.

Because the administration department also was made accountable for service to other groups, it worked very effectively with the terminal people, who were now also accountable for their costs, for improving the data-transmission system, and for cutting its cost. This was another area in which joint accountability was practiced.

The accounting department also was analyzed from the results viewpoint. To make sure that it caught any errors in the paperwork, the department had been checking and double checking a great deal without comparing the result obtained by this extra checking to the cost involved and to the slower service resulting to the regional personnel. Under such a system, too many items that could be handled at a lower level had tended to go up the line, resulting in slower handling and higher cost.

The first step was defining accounting's job to be that of general auditor rather than that of verifier of minutia. This was an attempt to cut "overcontrol" as illustrated by forms with spaces for "prepared by," checked by," and "approved by."

The head of administration was made accountable for value received from his records, and the cost of his record system was carefully scrutinized from this point of view. The whole program was then discussed with the home office staff, which took a very enlightened view and allowed some latitude in standard company practice in order to meet the problems faced in the region. As a consequence, a considerable reduction in administrative staff was realized, with an improvement in service to the regional people.

What were the overall gains from results management?

Three years after the installation of results management, the profit contribution of the region had gone up' about 35 percent. Among the more immediate results was an appreciable reduction in personnel, although this was actually secondary to the main objective.

The primary purpose of results management is to increase the return from the abilities that the firm has.

The overall application of results management to this region was begun by clarifying the goals of the region as tied to those of the company. It attempted to gear all the management people to these goals by looking at organization, policy, mode of adminstration, and accountability systems. Each management job was carefully scrutinized to determine whether it was directed to results that best contributed to the overall requirements of the region. It was recognized that each job might have contributions to make that were different from those of other jobs that were similar, because the problems faced by each were different. With firmer accountability for results set up for each job, authority was broadened. The new setup then allowed the region to better capitalize on the latent talents of its personnel in terms of real company results.

A keystone of the effort was the application of the joint accountability, securing a closer working relationship between staff and line personnel in the region. When staff is accountable for line results, it actually gives better service to the line and focuses less on activities of questionable value.

Finally, it was recognized that supervision was critical—especially at the first level. At this level, where training is most important, supervisors were given thorough instruction in how to train and were encouraged to follow through to upgrade and actually make their people successful. In the last analysis, then, company results improved at the same time as each person increased his capabilities.

DEMAND BETTER RESULTS—AND GET THEM

ROBERT H. SCHAFFER

One of the most dramatic large-scale productivity improvements with which I am familiar occurred in a regulated public utility—an industry category not noted for such performance breakthroughs. In the early 1960s this company's productivity was about average among 20 similar companies in North America, as both work load and work force were rapidly rising. In 1966 the trend shifted: the

Reprinted from *Harvard Business Review*. 52 November-December 1974: pp. 91-98 by permission of the author and publisher. © 1974 by the President and Fellows of Harvard College, all rights reserved.

work load continued to rise, but the number of employees began to drop. By 1968 the company's productivity ranked about the best in its industry. The difference between average performance and best was worth savings of more than $40 million a year—well over one third of its net income at that time.

What produced this gain? Neither new technology nor labor-saving machinery was a significant factor. No major change of management took place. The company was not reorganized. Nor were programs incorporating management by objectives, organization development, mathematical modeling, or management information systems responsible for the shift. The key to the turnaround was a decision by the principal operating officer (with backing from the chief executive) that the company must and could make substantial productivity gains. Naturally, many supportive programs and activities were necessary to translate this determination into results. These activities, however, would have produced little in the absence of a clear demand for improved performance that was placed on the company's management team.

Most organizations have the potential for as great—or greater—gains. Very few, however, ever realize them. Why? Because few managers possess the capacity—or feel compelled—to establish high performance improvement expectations in ways that elicit results. Indeed, the capacity for such demand making could be the most universally underdeveloped management skill.

WHY DEMANDS AREN'T MADE

Pushing for major gains can appear very risky to managers, and these perceived risks exert a tremendous inhibition on performance expectations. If the newly installed manager asserts that major gains are possible, he may threaten his predecessor and his current boss—and thus arouse their antagonism—by implying that they were content with less than what is possible. Even if he has been in the job for awhile, he subjects himself to the same criticism.

Great demands increase the risk of resistance from subordinates, and the possible embarrassment of setting ambitious goals and failing to reach them. The manager who sets unusually high demands may be challenged by others. He must therefore be sure of his facts and clear about directions. The struggle to upgrade performance may expose his uncertainties, weaknesses, and inadequate knowledge. More modest expectations reduce all these risks.

In addition, establishing well-defined and unequivocal expectations for superior performance creates the worry that failure of subordinates to produce will call for drastic action. The vice-president of a manufacturing operation recently mused out loud about a long-needed productivity improvement effort. "What would happen," he asked, "if we set specific targets and my people didn't meet them? I'd have to *do* something—maybe let some of them go. Then I'd have to bring in people I trusted even less." Before determining whether he could create an effective strategy, this man was already paralyzed by the anticipated consequences of failure.

The fear of rejection is also a powerful motivator. Asking subordinates to do much more than they assert they can do runs the risk, at least in a manager's mind, of earning their resentment, if not their dislike. Many managers have been only too eager to adopt the model of the manager portrayed by the human relations movements of the 1950s and 1960s—the loving, understanding, and supportive father figure. The stern, demanding father model was portrayed as a villain.

Although many exponents of "human relations" did emphasize the importance of high expectations and tough goals, managers frequently overlooked those parts of the message. Instead, they saw that high expectations for performance could lead to psychological rejection by subordinates. Prevailing opinion seemed to suggest that by adopting the right techniques managers could avoid confronting subordinates on performance expectations and asking them to produce much more than the managers estimated they would be likely to obtain from these subordinates anyhow.

Psychological Camouflage

Are managers conscious of the discrepancy between the performance they are requiring and what might be possible? To an extent, they are. Most sense that their organizations could achieve more, but their vision is obstructed. To avoid the uneasiness and feelings of guilt produced by too clear a vision of the performance gaps, managers unconsciously employ a variety of psychological mechanisms for obstructing the truth.

Avoidance through Rationalization. A manager may escape having to demand better performance by convincing himself that he has done all he can to establish expectations. For instance, he may assert that everyone already knows what must be accomplished. When asked whether he has made the goals clear to his people, he responds with a variation of: "If they don't know what the goals of this outfit are by now, they don't belong in their jobs."

Sincere in their belief that their subordinates are doing their best, managers frequently look for subpar performance elsewhere. Do the following statements sound familiar?

- "We can reduce back orders, but you're going to have to pay for plenty of overtime."
- "If you want us to cut inventories any further, be prepared for delayed shipments."
- "Ever since they trimmed our maintenance budget, we haven't been able to keep this plant operating properly."

Performance improvements always seem to call for an expansion of resources or an increase in authority. Overlooking the possibility of obtaining greater yields from available resources, managers often fail to impose greater demands and expectations on their employees. And when a manager does try to demand more, his subordinates are quick to point out that they are doing all that can be done. Thus all levels of management may share the illusion of operating at the outer limit when, in fact, they are far from it.

To avoid having to impose new requirements on subordinates, the manager may decide to take on the job himself. He reassures himself that his people are already overloaded or that they lack some qualification that he possesses.

At the other extreme is the manager who covers up his reluctance to make demands with toughness, gruffness, or arbitrariness. He may threaten or "needle" subordinates without actually specifying requirements and deadlines for results. In the folklore of management, such toughness of manner is equated with a preoccupation with achievement.

Reliance on Mechanisms and Procedures.   A manager may avoid the necessity of demand making by putting his chips on a variety of management programs, procedures, mechanisms, and innovations which he hopes will produce better results. They may help an organization respond to demands, but they are no substitute for good management.

For example, a manager may try an incentive system aimed at seducing subordinates into better performance through the promise of "goodies." Many top officers are perpetually preoccupied with new kinds of salary, profit-sharing, and stock-option plans and other so-called incentives like promotions, titles, and other per-quisites. The management assumes that if the right carrots are held out, managers and employees will run like rabbits.

Or infusions of new management technology may appear to be the key to performance improvements. Management will install information systems, mathematical planning models, industrial engineering studies, training programs, or any of dozens of other "programs" offered by technical staff or outside consultants. Top management may even reorganize the company—or parts of it. Even the best-trained staff technicians and management con-sultants—perhaps convinced of the magic in their medicines— become the unwitting co-conspirators of managers who fail to establish higher performance requirements for subordinates. In one well-known international company, an internal consulting group put together a mathematical planning model to maximize corporate profits in interdivisional negotiations. But the president used a flimsy excuse to escape from the struggle of requiring his division heads to operate within the framework of the models.

Attacks that Skirt the Target.   A manager may set tough goals and insist they be achieved—and yet fail to produce a sense of accounta-bility in subordinates. For example, managers often define goals— even significant ones—in vague or general terms that make ac-countability impossible. The R&D director is told that he "must get more new products out this year"; the personnel director hears that "turnover must be reduced"; the executives of a transportation company insist that "safety is our number one objective." When reporting time comes, who can say whether these objectives have been met?

Or the manager may establish goals but insist that he cannot hold a subordinate accountable for producing a result because the subordinate lacks the authority to get the job done. The case of a petrochemical plant whose product quality was well below par illustrates this point. Quality depended on how well a number of interdependent departments processed components. Top management charged department heads to improve operations and monitored these activities; but it failed to hold any individuals responsible for the quality of the end product on the grounds that none of them was in sufficient control of all the factors. The quality improvements failed to meet expectations.

Sometimes, when pressed by superiors, a manager will establish "expectations" in a way that communicates to subordinates that he is merely following instructions from above. In fact, he unconsciously hopes that his subordinates will fall short, "proving," as he has asserted all along, that the new stretch goals cannot be attained.

Ironically, management by objectives programs often create heavy paper snowstorms in which managers can escape from demand making. In many MBO programs, as the lists of goals get longer and the documents get thicker, the focus becomes diffused, bulk is confused with quality, and energy is spent on the mechanics rather than on results. A manager challenged on the performance of his group can safely point to the packet of papers and assert, "Every one of my managers has spent many hours developing his goals for the year."

STRATEGY FOR ACTION

The avoidance mechanisms just described act as powerful deterrents to major performance improvement—but they do not have to. There are ways to accelerate progress.

If you are convinced that you *must* achieve better results in your organizations* and you are willing to invest time and energy, you can learn to expect more and get more. I have seen the process work in a refinery that expanded its output while reducing its force by half; in a large urban teaching hospital that had to shift its mission

*See Larry E. Greiner 1967. Patterns of organization change. *Harvard Business Review* (May-June): p. 119, for data on the importance of pressures in generating performance improvement.

and direction radically; in a poorly maintained detergent and foodstuffs plant that had to become more competitive without more investment; and in school systems where determined leaders generated innovation despite the inertia of tradition.

The key to the strategy is to make an initial successful attempt at upgrading expectations and obtaining a response—and then use this achievement as the foundation for a succession of increasingly ambitious steps. A series of demands, initially limited, then more ambitious—each supported by careful plans, controls, and persistence—makes success more likely than does a big plunge involving demands for sweeping changes.

Step 1 Select the Goal.   You should start with an urgent problem, such as: Are the costs of one department too high? Is a budget being seriously overrun? Is a quality spec being consistently missed? Is there a shortfall in meeting a sales quota? You should begin with problems like these because it is essential to generate the feeling that achievement of the goal is imperative, not merely desirable.

As you are selecting the goal, you should assemble the information needed to frame the performance demand. You must have this information not only to define the need and specify the target, but possibly also to convince subordinates why improvement of performance is essential.

It is wise to sound out your subordinates on the opportunities for improvement. Their responses will give you a sense of their readiness as you shape your demand. By way of illustration, the management at a newspaper publishing plant tried to launch a comprehensive improvement effort. The needs were so great and resistance by managers at lower levels was so strong that very little was accomplished. Interviews with the composing room supervisors revealed that they shared higher management's distress over the number of typographical errors in news and advertising matter. This information provided the clue that made it possible to design an initial project mobilizing supporters of change.

The more participation by subordinates in determining goals, the better. Managers should not, however, permit their dedication to the participatory process to mean abdication of their own responsibilities in this determination.

Step 2 Specify the Minimum Expectation for Results.   Broad, far-reaching, or amorphous goals must be narrowed to one or two specific, measurable ones. A manager may protest with "I have too many things that have to get done to concentrate on only one or two of them." But the fragmentation of a manager's attention in trying to push them all ahead can keep him perpetually trapped in the same defense mechanisms from which he is trying to escape. Whether the first-step goal is a modest advance or a bold one, it must focus the energy of the organization on one or two sharply defined targets.

For example, one company, in treading a path between mass production and tailored engineering, was losing money because it could not clarify its proper place in the market and develop the appropriate products. Top management spent hundreds of hours in conferences and in making studies to define the business, the product line, and the pricing strategy. These produced more frustration than progress.

The undertaking was transformed, however, when the president asked the group to select, from a dozen being considered, the one new product the executives agreed would most likely be profitable and conform to their vision of the business. He directed them to sketch out a market plan and pricing policy for this product. They were to draw some generalizations from this effort which could be applied to policy determination. The president was convinced that the group could produce the result in a short time. And he was confident that the initial step would provide insights into the nature of the next steps in clarifying company directions.

Step 3 Communicate Your Expectations Clearly.   You should share with the responsible persons, orally and in writing, the determination of the goal, the locus of responsibility, the timetable, and the constraints. It is important to make clear that you are not asking for permission to set the goal, not securing their advice on whether the goal is attainable, and not implying that if they do not meet the target you will nevertheless appreciate their efforts. It should be clear that this is not a goal that *should* be achieved; it is one that *must* be achieved.

Step 4 Monitor the Project, but Delegate Responsibility.   The use of work-planning disciplines is essential in these projects to keep them from fading into the ether. Trying, for instance, to keep the goals, commitments, and plans only in your mind is sure to under-mine the project; rather, the manager responsible for each goal or subgoal should provide you with a written work plan of steps to be taken to reach the goal. This work plan should also specify how progress will be measured and how it will be reported to you.

Moreover, the responsibility for achieving each goal must be assigned to one person, although the contributions of many may be essential for success. Consider the case of a company whose techni-cally complex new product was failing to perform as promised. The president talked about the problem with his marketing, engineering and manufacturing vice-presidents; each claimed that his function was doing its job and that the problems originated elsewhere. After spending much more time than warranted with his subordinates, the president was able to effect only a slight improvement.

The turnaround came when he called together the department heads concerned and told them it was unwise for him to get involved in trying to solve the problem. That was *their* job. He was therefore giving full responsibility to them, he said, to come up with a plan to reduce the frequency of unacceptable products to a target level within three months. He assigned to one executive the responsibility for shaping an integrated plan and for making certain it was ade-quate to achieve the result. In addition, the president said that each of the other managers would have to produce a plan specifying his own functions, contributions, and timetable. After many months of struggling for a solution, these moves for the first time (1) pin-pointed a goal to be achieved, (2) established responsibilities for achievement, and (3) introduced work-planning disciplines to manage the process in an orderly way.

The frustrations experienced by this president demonstrate that as long as responsibility for results is not explicitly assigned, subordinates tend to "delegate" it to the boss, especially if he tries to play a helpful role in the project. The boss must make certain that his subordinates clearly understand their full responsibility for results. He must not permit them to seize his offers of help and support as an opportunity to pass the buck.

Step 5 Expand and Extend the Process. Once some success has been achieved on a first set of demands, it should be possible to repeat the process on new goals or on an extension of the first. This will lead to further expansion.

As an example, consider the efforts of a large railway express terminal that handled tens of thousands of shipments daily. It was performing very poorly on many counts: costs were high, productivity was low, and delivery deadlines were often missed. Studies had identified the potential for saving hundreds of thousands of dollars; but little had been achieved. Then the head of the terminal and his boss ceased talking about what was going wrong and all the improvements that were needed. Instead, they identified the most crucial short-term goals.

From these few they selected one: getting *all* of one category of shipments out on time each day. It was not an easy goal, but it was clear and understandable; it could be defined sharply and measured, and action steps could be quickly identified. Meeting that target was the all-important first success that launched the terminal on a major improvement program. Once the first traffic category was under control, top management planned a series of slightly more ambitious improvement programs. Gradually, the terminal's managers gained confidence in asking for more; and their subordinates gained confidence that they could respond. Eventually, many of the sizable savings promised in the earlier studies were realized.

PSYCHODYNAMICS OF ACTION

While moving ahead through successive sets of demands, top management has some essential work to do on the psychological front as well. The methods and procedures for negotiating goals with subordinates are well-known; almost overlooked, but more significant, are the often unconscious negotiations which the manager carries on with himself. A manager frequently bargains himself down to comfortable expectation levels long before he confronts his subordinates. He must learn to share the risk taking that he wants his subordinates to assume. He may have to live with the "testing" to which subordinates may subject him, and he may need to engage in "consciousness raising" to make sure he does not slip into rationalizations for failing to see that his directives are carried out.

Without intending to, a manager often ensures that he will share in the glories of his subordinates' successes, but that they will take the blame for failures. For example, a plant manager had been pressuring the head of maintenance to realign the responsibilities of supervisors and workers in order to increase efficiency. The step would make a number of persons redundant. Low-level managers and supervisors resisted the move, warning of various disasters that would befall the plant. The deadlock was broken only when the plant manager—through transfers, early retirements, and a very modest layoff—reduced the maintenance force to the level needed after the proposed reorganization. Now that the most painful step had been taken, maintenance management quickly installed the new structure. Instead of insisting self-righteously that the key to action was overcoming the resistance of maintenance management, the plant manager assumed the risk and broke the logjam by reducing the staff.

When the manager lets his subordinates know that he expects better results, they may express their own lack of self-confidence in the form of "tests." They may still do exactly what they have been doing, as if to say they heard his words but disbelieve the message. Or they may imply that "It can't be done." Some subordinates may advise him, dropping their voices confidentially, that for his own good—considering the high risks involved—he should lower his sights. They may even withdraw their affection and approbation from him.

Such testing is usually the expression of their anxiety over whether they can actually achieve the goal; it is a way to seek reassurance from the boss. If the boss is as anxious as they are, he will be upset by the testing and he may react against what he perceives as defiance. If he has confidence in himself, he will accept the testing for what it is and try to help his subordinates deal with the problem—without, however, eroding his expectation levels.

In breaking out of productiveness-limiting traps, "consciousness raising" may be needed to help managers assess more objectively their approach to establishing demands. Consultants—inside or outside—can help managers gain the necessary perspective. Or several managers who are working through the same process may join forces, since each can be more detached about the others' behavior than about his own. They may meet periodically to probe such questions as: Have you adequately assessed the potential for progress? Have you made the performance requirements clear to your associates? Are these goals ambitious enough? Are you providing your subordinates with enough help? Are you sharing the risks with them? How well are you standing up to "testing?" Have you defined goals that at least some of your subordinates can see as exciting and achievable?

Perhaps the most important function of consciousness raising has to do with getting started in the first place. It is very difficult to alter the pattern of relationships involving superior and subordinate, especially if they have been working together for a long time. You cannot take the very first step without worrying that your people may say (or think), "Oh, come off it, Bob. We know who you are!"

THE REWARDS ARE THERE

The strategy for demanding better performance—and getting it—begins with a focus on one or two vital goals. Management assesses readiness and then sharply defines the goal. The organization receives clearly stated demands and unequivocally stated expectations. Management assigns the responsibility for results to individuals, and work-planning discipline provides the means for self-control and assessment of progress. Management keeps wired in, tenaciously, making sure the project moves. Early successes provide the reinforcement to shoot for more ambitious targets, which may be extensions of the first goal or additional goals.

There is no limit to the pace or scope of expansion. As this process expands, a shift in management style and organizational dynamics gradually takes place. Sophisticated planning techniques, job redesign, closer line/staff collaboration, and other advances result as natural developments of the process.

With clearly conveyed "nonnegotiable" expectations and a step-by-step expansion strategy, you may find that the anticipated difficulties and dangers fail to materialize. Instead, if your subordinates are like most, they will respond to the higher demands. They will be able to accomplish what is expected—or most of it. And, despite a bit of "testing" or hazing, most of them will enjoy working in a more results-oriented environment. Thus you will be creating an environment in which there is more job satisfaction, greater mutual respect, and better relationships among levels—as well as a multiplied return on the organization's human and material resources.

PUTTING IT ALL TOGETHER FOR
ORGANIZATIONAL EFFECTIVENESS [1]

Perhaps the most distinctive characteristic of our approach to MBO/R is the emphasis that is placed on achieving organization RESULTS through organizational effectiveness. This does not occur through individual achievement nearly so much as it does through people working *together* in groups or teams as part of a larger system. There is considerable literature which deals with how to write objectives, but the leading edge of MBO technology seems to be concerning itself with applications at the human level in a group context.

THE HUMAN SIDE OF ORGANIZATION RESULTS

When individuals function in teams or groups (subsystems) to produce organization RESULTS through a goal setting process, they are into the human side of RESULTS. Managing and working in this context can be quite demanding. But it is here, with the people in the organization, where we really make MBO/R work by managing the process of human relationships. MBO/R, OD, and all other technology come together within the individual person. How each person perceives reality will have a marked effect on that person's success or failure in the organization.

In order to manage this approach, we need to develop some different perceptions of the process of management and the organization. The increasing application of behavioral science technology and its integration with MBO/R using an organizational focus is moving many people into new dimensions of organization life. One quickly comes to grips with the need to think and conceptualize at the "whole" or "holistic" level. In this situation you have to be able to move almost instantly from a level of concern for the whole organization to a level of concern for the whole individual as described in Chapter 5 relative to figure and ground perception using the illustration of the vase and silhouetted profiles. It is also like listening and responding to the vibration of a symphony orchestra or a Dixieland band while at the same time being able to identify with an instrument in first one section, then another.

To make MBO/R work in this context we must be willing—individually and organizationally—to develop our understanding and skills in these areas:

1) our way of thinking, feeling, and behaving
2) the normative values that we hold and how our own valuing occurs
3) group and process (how we work together) technology needed to implement objective writing skills including things like:

   a. planning,
   b. problem solving,
   c. managing the helping relationship, differences, and accountability.[2]

WORKING WITH A SYSTEMS APPROACH

Our colleague, Richard S. Underhill, has developed a way of visualizing the interrelationship of five major areas of interest which contribute to developing an effective organization. Figure 6.1 shows the linking of MBO/R, OD, human resources, human systems, and emPOWERment. Having the focus on organization RESULTS, we are able to use the idea of "think systems" to constantly validate that we are considering the What, How, and Who relative to the whole system or any subsystem.

In this and earlier chapters we have dealt with various aspects of these areas. Some clarification of human resources and human

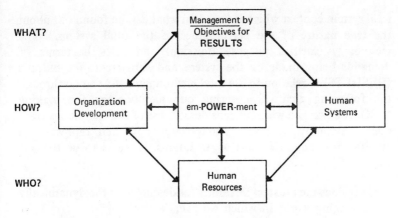

Fig. 6.1 Entry points for diagnosis and planning.

systems might be helpful here. The area of human resources deals with the individual, personal values, and personal growth. These are the things that develop and affirm the self-concept of the person within his work group and organization. Within the framework of human systems we are seeking to ensure that the supportive systems of the organization are responsive to human needs. Such systems would be concerned with developing policies, procedures, structures, and operations that were supportive of individuals in achieving organization RESULTS.

In the evolution of our approach to making MBO/R work, we have drawn heavily on open system technology as applied to sociotechnical systems or human organizations. As we experimented with various approaches that were supportive of our humanistic and process orientation, these were the things that worked. Much of the applied open system technology is supportive of our approach to planning and developing the navigation system described in later chapters. At the end of this chapter you will find Partin's "Emerging Perspectives about Organization Planning and Development" which describes and compares open and closed system approaches.

The open system approach takes a holistic or whole view rather than a partial view. It seeks to place the output of a subsystem into a total system context which is based on what can be found out about the true nature of the performance of the total system.[3] The technology clarifies purpose (mission) and roles in terms of demands being made on the system and subsystems for outputs (RESULTS) in relation to the total environment. As you go through the following chapters covering our methodology for making MBO/R work, you will find considerable use of the techniques from open system applications. Though this approach represents a significant change for most organizations, it seems to be the one which:

- provides the greatest flexibility for dealing with the dynamically changing world in which we live,
- focuses on organization (system) RESULTS (outputs),
- is fully supportive of maximum human growth, and
- develops a management style that is responsive to what is happening in the organization "now."

These first six chapters have covered various issues that are basic to managing the goal setting process in such a way as to make MBO/R work. Unless an organization or team is consciously working with these issues, it is doubtful, in our approach especially, that they will achieve much long term success relative to organization RESULTS.

The chapters that follow provide the steps for implementing our approach to <u>Management</u> by Objectives for RESULTS. Before you ever get to actually writing objectives, there is much to be done in developing the organization's navigation system and a broad base of planning data. With that direction to guide the organization, the setting of objectives by both organizational units and individuals tends to be much more productive. Chapters 7 to 15 provide detailed implementation suggestions for each step, and Chapter 16 deals with specific skills and competencies which will be required.

When this approach has been implemented and the various aspects integrated with a balance between the individual and organizational needs, you will have it all together for organization effectiveness and RESULTS.

NOTES

1. Some of the thoughts in this chapter were part of a presentation given at the Second Annual International conference on "MBO: State of the Art" in August 1974. A modified version of that presentation has been published in the April 1975 issue of the *Training and Development Journal* with the title Where OD and MBO meet. Extracts are used herein with their permission.

2. In Chapter 16 we elaborate on various skills and competencies that are needed to work with MBO/R.

3. L.H. Mantell 1972. The systems approach and good management, *Business Horizons*, (October), p. 44.

EMERGING PERSPECTIVES ABOUT ORGANIZATION PLANNING AND DEVELOPMENT

J. JENNINGS PARTIN

Earliest man saw a need for organizations. Anthropologists have documented the nature of human organizations that developed early in the evolution of civilized man. The need for organized groups is no less today than ever before. How they function however is changing rapidly and becoming increasingly more difficult to manage.

The increasing number of meetings on organization planning and development is evidence of increasing interest in the nature of organization in a complex environment. This interest is not based on idle curiosity so much as it is survival in a rapidly changing world.

STATE OF TURMOIL

We live in an age of discontinuity. However, the nature of social change is such that there are always holdovers from the past. These exist alongside new behavior patterns which are established. Still newer ways of viewing things are expressed. The net effect of all this is a state of continual turmoil which is difficult for individuals and organizations to cope with.

First, let us examine some of the underlying assumptions and concepts of prevailing organization theory and note some of the problems they encounter in today's environment. Second, we will examine stages in the evolution of organization design and the values on which they are based. Third, we will study the process of value formation and its effects on organization. We will then look at the effects of social change on traditional organization concepts. Finally, we will consider an approach to organization which appears to be a viable alternative to traditional models as a means of dealing with the emerging social environment.

TRADITIONAL ORGANIZATION ASSUMPTIONS

The principles of "scientific management" which were articulated by Frederick Taylor are well known. We've all been perplexed by the problems of living with organization objectives, line/staff relationships, chain of command, span of control, responsibility/authority relationships, and other traditional guidelines for organization design and functioning.

These are all based on a rather interesting set of assumptions about what the character of organizations should be. It seems fair to describe the thinking of traditional organization theory in the following ways:

1. The structure of an organization is determined by a rational thought process intended to control the organization in order to achieve its end.

2. The basis for functional designations is commonality of purpose.

3. Objectives and goals are formally stated in order to openly express the purpose of the organization.

4. Organizational hierarchy presupposes a differential jurisdiction over people and a delegation of specific tasks to a particular unit.

5. Decentralization allows for specialized entrepreneurial functions without loss of efficiency or control.

6. The basic aim of the entrepreneurial functions is the welfare of the organization and its continued viability.

7. The organization is designed to achieve the least cost or greatest return for management/stockholders.

8. Optimal solutions to solving an organization problem can be achieved by discovering a better way to operate the formal model.

9. Organizational tasks are viewed as recurring cycles, viewed in terms of patterns.

10. Checks and balances are imperative.

11. A routine, specialized information system is mandatory.

12. Management action is directly related to information the system provided.

Much more can be said about the typical pyramidal, hierarchical, bureaucratic model that characterizes typical organization models. They are designed for endurance and are a product of the conventional wisdom that prevailed in a much more stable environment than we find in the 1970s.

ORGANIZATION DESIGN DEVELOPMENT

A stable world, however, has never existed. Consequently, organization design was modified through the years as new insights were gained. There appears to be a discernable pattern of design changes that accompanies changes in environment. Organizations can be classified into three categories although variations are found in each type.

Organization according to function centralized or multifunctional organization developed during the 1920s and is still widely used. The basic organizing principle is to group similar activities under major functional managers who, in turn, report to central headquarters (Fig. 1).

The next form to appear was a decentralized divisional or multidivisional organization (Fig. 2). This idea was pioneered by

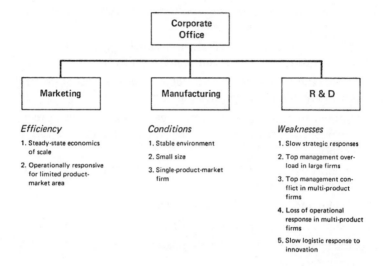

Fig. 1 Functional organization design.*

GM and DuPont. The basic principle of this form is to group activities by related product-markets and not by related activities. Each division is assigned to a manager who has complete responsibility for the strategic, administrative and operational decisions in areas assigned to him.

Increasing problems with the functional and divisional forms has led to some recent adaptations which have in effect created substantially different organization forms. Many companies since World War II and especially in the defense industry have gone to a matrix organization or project management design. The principle behind these designs is to form temporary organizations with sufficient authority, responsibility, and resources to serve a specific product-market with a limited life cycle (Fig. 3).

The manager of one of these organizations "Owns" a number of people of various skills and utilizes others on a temporary basis as needed. The latter remain *functionally* responsible to a manager in

*H.I. Ansoff and R.G. Brandenburg 1971. A language for organization design. *Management Science* 17, 12, (August).

another organization but are *administratively* responsible to the project manager during the time of his service there.

Organization design has gone through a number of stages. Each form is suited to certain conditions. Its effectiveness decreases as environmental conditions change. That in short is where the basic source of organizational stress comes from today. Stability is gone. Flux and change are constant. The thrust of our current social upheaval is directed toward the established units of our society.

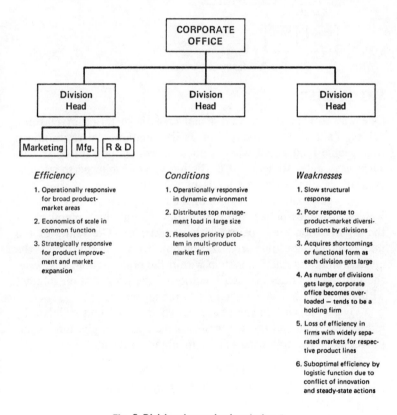

Efficiency

1. Operationally responsive for broad product-market areas
2. Economics of scale in common function
3. Strategically responsive for product improvement and market expansion

Conditions

1. Operationally responsive in dynamic environment
2. Distributes top management load in large size
3. Resolves priority problem in multi-product market firm

Weaknesses

1. Slow structural response
2. Poor response to product-market diversifications by divisions
3. Acquires shortcomings or functional form as each division gets large
4. As number of divisions gets large, corporate office becomes overloaded — tends to be a holding firm
5. Loss of efficiency in firms with widely separated markets for respective product lines
6. Suboptimal efficiency by logistic function due to conflict of innovation and steady-state actions

Fig. 2 Divisional organization design.*

Ibid.

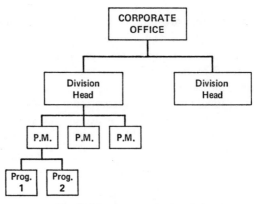

Fig. 3 Adaptive organization design.*

VALUE BASE

One way to view the current social crisis is in terms of clashing values. Values can be thought of as the fundamental assumptions that people hold about what is good or evil, important or trivial. They are guides to action. Conflicting values evoke personal confrontations at the deepest levels of one's being.

In organizations, the values of the management affect its style. Values influence policy, the boundaries within which members of the organization may operate without restraint. The values of top management determine organization objectives. They influence the entire human interaction system within the organization. Likewise, the individual values of each member of the organization interact with the prevailing attitudes of the management.

Over time, certain values are viewed as sacred and inviolate by management in traditional organizations. For example, most companies hold the following values in highest esteem:

1. Activism: It is better to appear active than idle.

2. Optimism: The future will be better than today. We are growing and expanding.

3. Egalitarianism: Opportunity is widespread for all. We are an equal opportunity employer (i.e., EEO). There is upward mobility in our company.

*Ibid.

4. Practicability: Actions should be chosen on a practical basis.*

These basic core values are then translated into organization goals, found in various policies, procedures and objectives. These concepts become a part of the very fabric that the management works with in achieving organizational goals. They are the core of the ideal image the company wants for itself, and are often articulated like this:

1. *Effectiveness*: We want to become increasingly effective in successfully coping with organizational problems.

2. *Growth*: We want to grow in size and scope, and continuously improve our technical competence and quality.

3. *Realization of Potential*: We want to realize our potential competence and organizational power.

4. *Productivity:* We want to continuously increase the ratio of output of goods or services to the input of human energy, money, and materials.

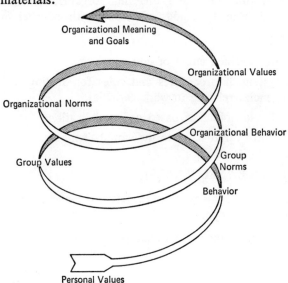

Fig. 4 Effects of values and norms in organizations.

*A.H. Kuriloff 1972. *Organization development for survival.* New York: American Management Association.

5. *Social Image*: We want to be viewed as being socially useful and beneficial to the community (e.g., ecology).*

These values are consistent with the Protestant Ethic which gave impetus to the industrial revolution. They are found in every organization. They have a unique configuration in each organization based on the personal values of its members. An interaction occurs between the organization and the individual. The effects of that interaction affect the achievement of both organizational and individual objectives. (See Fig. 4.)

Typical pyramidal, hierarchical organizations resist variance from norms. They tend to deny individual differences. In a time of radical change, value confrontations are inevitable.

EFFECTS OF SOCIAL CHANGE

Some basic components of traditional organizations follow. The traditional functional and divisional organization models have rather well-defined methods of dealing with external forces.

They have:

1. A well-defined chain of command.
2. A system of procedures and rules for dealing with all contingencies relating to work activities.
3. A division of labor based on specialization.
4. Uniform approaches to individual members.

DISRUPTIVE INFLUENCES†

Organizations of this type are threatened whenever one or more of the following happens:

1. Rapid and unexpected change.

Ibid.

†W.G. Bennis 1969. Organization development: its nature, origin, and prospects. In E. Schein, W. Bennis, and R. Beckhard (eds.), *Addison-Wesley Series on Organization Development*, 6 vols.

2. Growth in size where the volume of the organization's traditional activities is not enough to sustain growth.

3. Complexity of modern technology where integration between activities and persons of very diverse, highly specialized competence is required.

4. A psychological threat springs from a change in organizational behavior.*

These threats can be analyzed in terms of internal and external forces. The *external* forces have been identified by social scientists. It is difficult for us to understand what is happening to our society because we are too much a part of what is happening. We are at the same time participants and observers of a drama whose plot is being created as it is being played. No one is singularly responsible for its development.

However, some aspects of what is happening can be identified. Our culture is in a state of disequilibrium. Individually, we are unable to assimilate impending change quickly enough.

In a recent three-year period, 66 of the top 100 companies reported major reorganizations. The need for more information quicker has undermined traditional structures. The stable organizations of the past have been unable to remain the same.

CHANGE, STRESS IN PHILOSOPHIES

Changes in the thinking of society at large have affected the thinking or people inside the organization. New management philosophies are emerging to combat traditional ones. At least six theories worthy of mention contribute to our "jungle."†

1. *Management Process school:* This theory speaks of functions required for effective management—planning, organizing, staffing, directing, and controlling. The idea here is that if you teach and execute these functions well, the enterprise will be successful.

*Ibid.
†Kuriloff, *op. cit.*

2. *Decision Theory school:* This school says that management practice rests in making good decisions. The best decisions are based on the rational choice from among alternatives. If people are trained in decision making, the whole organization will function more effectively.

3. *Mathematical school:* The key to effective management is to produce mathematical models and processes which indicate the way an organization should move. Operations research has gained prestige because of this emphasis.

4. *Empirical school (reconstructionist):* Effective management of any organization can be best accomplished by identifying and implementing the successful practices of the past. The organization is preserved by maintaining the style of management that made it what it is.

5. *Social System school:* This theory views the organization as a social system comprising various groups working toward common purposes. The task of management is to develop a macro-system unique to its organization. In this way coordination, open communication, and effective personal transactions will be assured.

6. *Human Behavior school:* This is in contrast to, but not in conflict with, the social system approach. This school is a micro-approach focusing on the quality of relationships among the members of the organization. Good managers are expected to develop interpersonal competence and utilize this in increasing collaboration at all levels and groups throughout the organization.

The first four theories—management process, decision theory, mathematical, and empirical—are of classical derivation. They express the values of "scientific management." The last two—social system and human behavior—are based on recent insights gained from the social and behavioral sciences, primarily sociology and psychology. The former group attempts to achieve a neat, orderly, predictable management climate. The latter two value open, democratic, participative methods that are typically not very neat or as predictable.

The crisis all organizations are facing can be directly attributed to the internal and external forces we've mentioned briefly. The challenge is to attain a balance which enables the best insights from each approach to influence the organization. The *prevailing management style,* its values, *the structure of the organization,* its assumptions, and the *quality of personal relationships,* their effects, all determine the viability of any organization. The task then is how to understand the environment, the organization, and the human system to determine *what is* and *what ought to be* and to find an effective way to make the transition.

THE SYSTEMS CONCEPT

Thus far we have looked at how things got to be the way they are from one person's perspective. We've referred to the typical hierarchical organization (functional or divisional) as being traditional and based on the classical assumptions about the nature of organization and the nature of man. We've also examined some of the threats these established views are experiencing in terms of changes in societal values.

Let us now look at an approach to understanding organizations that appears to deal with rapid change more effectively. It is based on some different assumptions and allows for the existence of varying values inside and outside the system.

CLOSED AND OPEN SYSTEMS

Developments in the biological sciences and electronics have made it possible to adapt some of their models for organizations. Systems theory as applied to organizations can classify organizations as closed or open systems. A simple system's model consists of input, processing, and output. If you add a feedback mechanism from output to input, you have an example of a *closed system* (e.g., thermostat).

Traditional organization models (functional, divisional) are examples of closed systems. The adaptive organization models are examples of open systems.

Closed systems are described in terms of the *second law* of *thermodynamics*. The system moves toward equilibrium. It tends to run down. Its differentiated structures tend to move toward dissolution. A second descriptive term identified with a closed system is *entropy*. Entropy increases toward a maximum. Equilibrium occurs as the system attains the state of the most probable distribution of its elements.

In other words, the structure of the organization becomes increasingly fixed and rigid, more difficult to change. *A priori* assumptions go unchallenged. The *Peter principle* unconsciously affects manpower planning.

OPEN SYSTEMS' CHARACTERISTICS

At this point it is probably helpful to investigate the concepts of open systems theory.*

1. *Importation of Energy:* Every individual is dependent on the continuous inflow of stimulation from the external environment. Likewise, organizations must draw energy (human and inanimate) from outside sources in order to perform their tasks.

2. *Through-put:* Open systems transform the energy that is available to them. The organization creates a product, processes materials, trains people, or provides a service (i.e., some work gets done).

3. *Out-put:* Open systems export some product into the environment.

4. *Systems as Cycles of Events:* The pattern of activities of the energy exchange has a cyclic character. A system can be identified whenever an interrelated set of events returns upon itself to complete or renew a cycle of activities. Events rather than things are structured, so that the organization structure is *dynamic* rather than *static*. Activities or behavior are structured so that they comprise a *unity in their completion or closure*.

*D. Katz and R.L. Kahn 1966. *The social psychology of organizations.* New York: Wiley.

A single cycle of events of a self-closing character gives a single form of structure. Single cycles combine to give a larger structure of events or an *event system.* Event systems may be composed of smaller cycles which are integral components of other systems not a part of the particular event system under consideration.

5. *Negative Entropy:* To survive, open systems must arrest the entropic process (i.e., acquire negative entropy). The entropic process is a universal law of nature which says that all forms of organization move toward disorganization or death. An open system can import *more* energy from its environment than it expends, and thus can store energy and acquire negative entropy (e.g. manpower planning, management development, recruitment).

6. *Information Input, Negative Feedback and the Coding Process: Inputs* into living systems consist of more than energy. Information furnishes signals to the organization about the environment and about its functioning relationship to the environment.

   Negative feedback is the simplest form of information the system receives. It enables it to correct its course. Without negative feedback there is no corrective action taken. Lacking this, the system will expend its energy, or ingest too much energy and the system will terminate.

   The *coding process* of the system selects which inputs will be absorbed into the system. This mechanism is determined by the nature of the functions performed by the system.

7. *The Steady State and Dynamic Homeostasis:* The importation of energy to arrest entropy operates to maintain some constancy in energy exchange, so that open systems that survive are characterized by a steady state.

   A steady state is a continuous flow of energy from the external environment and a continuous export of the products of the system, but the character of the system, the ratio of energy exchanges, and the relations between parts remains the same.

   Any internal or external factor which disrupts the system is countered by forces which restore the system as quickly as possible to its previous state.

Homeostasis is apparently contradictory to the tendency of living systems to grow and expand to counteract entropy. The basic tendency of the system is homeostatic in that it will *preserve its character*. Under stress the system will import more energy than needed for preserving its character. It acquires a margin of safety beyond the immediate level of existence. Social systems tend to incorporate within their boundaries the external resources essential to survival (i.e., the expansion of the original system;) (e.g., hoarding, over-staffing—as an amoeba).

At the simplest level, the steady state is homeostasis over time. At complex levels, the steady state is maintained by preserving the character of the system through growth and expansion (e.g., adding more units of the same essential type it already has).

8. *Differentiation:* Open systems move in the pattern of differentiation and elaboration. Diffuse global patterns are replaced by more specialized functions. Systems are first governed by dynamic interaction of their components; later on, fixed arrangements and conditions of constraint are established which render the system and its parts more efficient (e.g., policies, procedures).

9. *Equifinality:* A system can reach the same final state from differing initial conditions and by a variety of paths. As open systems move toward regulatory mechanisms to control their operations, the amount of equifinality may be reduced.

IMPLICATIONS OF SYSTEMS THEORY

Some subtle distinctions are to be made if systems theory is to be applied to organizations.

Closed systems are by definition those which tend to concentrate on their own internal functioning as if environmental changes were largely independent of the productivity, morale, and motivation of the organization. Coordination and control become ends in themselves rather than means to an end. Internal changes are viewed more in terms of attaining desired organizational goals rather than adjusting to the environment in order to achieve their objectives.

Closed systems tend to prescribe one best way for behaving because the conditions are already established each time a known problem occurs. Variances tend to call for full-scale investigations of the organization with incidental reference to environmental influences. *Open systems* on the other hand give extensive consideration to the interface between the organization and its environment. They are evolutionary, dynamic systems which adopt a positive stance on change.

THE SOCIO-TECHNICAL SYSTEM

Let us now shift from the theoretical underpinnings of systems theory to some applications of the theory for purposes of organization planning and development. In this context an industrial organization can be viewed as a socio-technical system. The simple input-process-output model is made more definitive. Systems processes are further delineated into transformation subsystems—goals and values, technology, structure, psycho-social, and managerial (Fig. 5).

Each subsystem is essential to the successful accomplishment of the organization's mission. Subsystems can be defined with sufficient properties that the internal processing of inputs can be improved so that eventual outputs can be affected.

1. *Goals and values subsystem:* Organization norms and personal values can be integrated by process interventions into the system (i.e., how things are done is important).

2. *Technology subsystem:* The technology of an organization refers to its knowledge and skills utilized in performing its tasks. This subsystem converts spontaneous and unreflective behavior into deliberate and rationalized behavior according to the technology the business employs.

3. *Structural subsystem:* Structure is the established pattern of relationships among the components or parts of the organiza-

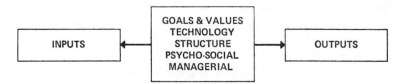

Fig. 5 Organization as a socio-technical system.*

tion. This is designed according to the concepts utilized by the organization. Traditional organizations focus on line/staff, span of control, chain of command and other classical principles of organization. A systems approach would design the structure according to the unique properties of the system under consideration.

4. *Psycho-social subsystem:* This system refers to the individual in social relationships. It can be understood in terms of the motivation and behavior occurring in environment which includes: status and role systems, group dynamics, influence systems, and leadership.

5. *Managerial subsystem:* This system views the ways managers coordinate work (1) through people, (2) via techniques, (3) in the organization, and (4) toward its objectives. It is the process by which human and material resources are integrated into the organization for accomplishing its objectives. This can be viewed in terms of (1) decision making, (2) control and influence, (3) recruitment processes, (4) orientation processes, (5) reward systems and (6) leadership.†

A SYSTEMS CHANGE AND ORGANIZATIONAL RENEWAL APPROACH

If one can accept a systems model of an organization, there are some logical extensions of this approach which affect the means by which systems are to be changed and renew themselves.

One of the basic assumptions regarding all organisms is that they remain healthy and survive to the extent that they develop the

*R.A. Schmuck and M.B. Miles 1971. *Organization development in schools.* Palo Alto, Calif.: National Press.
†*Ibid.*

capacity to develop effective integrations with their environments. This is especially important in the social context organizations are in today.

Following are requisites of a systems approach to change and renewal:*

1. *Determining environmental influences:* This is a repetitive process for helping the client group develop a contextual mapping of the manner in which it is currently interacting with its environment.

2. *Systems planning:* The main aim of this procedure is to recognize the demands of the environment and identify the responses the organization makes based on its value system.

3. *Systems design or redesign:* The purpose of this task is to help the client system organize itself so that it has the in-built dynamic capacity to make continual integrations with its changing environment.

   The result of this approach is that the client develops an integrated sense of what its present engagement with its environment looks like.

IDENTIFYING PROCESS

The process of identifying and defining the appropriate systems model is as follows:†

1. Identify the system's *core process*. What is the system trying to do? What is the nature of our business? What is the character of what we're trying to create or produce? What needs in the greater environment are we trying to answer?

   The core process contains the essential properties of the system.

2. The next stage is *environmental scanning*. This is identifying the external forces influencing the system. It is a process of making judgments about the realities at work in the inter-

*C. G. Krone 1971. Unpublished paper presented at the NTL New Technology in Organization Development Conference, New York.
†*Ibid.*

actions between the external environment and the internal world of the system.

This should be done as objectively as possible, while realizing the innate subjectivity of the identification process.

3. Identify demands made on the core. When done in a group, the demands vary—shared, conflicting, and independent. These "demand domains" define the requirements of the system.

4. Map out the inside responses to the system to each of the demand domains.

For every demand there is a response. The task is to identify particular responses. Frequently there are incongruities between the demand and the response. The effect on the client group is one of increasing self-awareness.

5. Identify ways to increase the congruity between the demand and the response.

Steps 1–4 are definition stages. Step 5 is a planning phase.

Responses to the demands can be prioritized to the values of the system. Temporary teams can be formed to develop plans for dealing with discrete processes within the system.

Here in capsule form is a technique for identifying the components of a system. The system can be the total organization, a major unit, or a unit of any scope depending on how the system is defined.

This approach offers flexibility in organization planning and development. It is contextual, uniquely suited to the system under study. The process has the added benefit of involving the client group in the system design and the planning it requires. It develops insight into the nature of the organization and its environment. During the process, values and norms of the organization are surfaced and accounted for in any strategies that are taken.

EMERGING PERSPECTIVES

The open systems approach seems to effectively answer the fluctuating, often conflicting demands made in today's social climate. Alvin Toffler documented some of these in his book *Future Shock.**

---

*A. Toffler 1970. *Future Shock.* New York: Bantam.

He noted forces which have deluged every human institution. With regard to organizations, two significant changes can be mentioned: (1) increased transiency and (2) changed views on the nature of human resources. The effects of changes in both of these realms are indicative of a need for an open systems approach to viewing organizations.

The effects of *Future Shock*, the disequilibrium found in persons influenced by change quicker than they can assimilate it, has created an ideology of *transience*. Social mobility has made it possible for people to move quickly, frequently, and great distances. Recruitment and employment efforts are vital to an organization's survival. Frequent job changes are not viewed as about career development and self-fulfillment than to organizational loyalty.

HUMAN RESOURCE FACTOR

Views toward *human resources* are also being affected. The "organization man," though once desired, is no longer a realistic expectation in most companies. People themselves are coming to accept employment changes as being inevitable. Frequently, these changes are made in order to do more interesting work than for financial considerations alone. This suggests increased independence on the part of the worker.

It appears that the values and assumptions of a closed, traditional system cannot long survive in the emerging social system. Organizations will be forced to become more participative. An open systems theory of organization planning and development is suited to meet unexpected demands in an efficient and effective manner. It has the capacity for enabling the organization to realistically view itself and its environment and start the long process of becoming what it wants to be, must be.

MBO/R NAVIGATION AND
OPERATION SYSTEMS

In Chapter 1 the managing for RESULTS aspects of the MBO/R concept were emphasized. To achieve this it is helpful to have some structure in the tasks that have to be managed. The MBO/R Navigation and Operation System[1] (Fig. 7.1) could be called a step-by-step approach, but we prefer not to do this because the steps may be taken out of order and an organization may start at different points depending on the most pressing problems at a given point in time.

This MBO/R navigation system will make managers aware of the issues that have to be resolved in an organization before objectives should be written. Many organizations start MBO/R by writing objectives when the mission, roles, and RESULTS areas are not clear or unidentified. Quite often these objectives are written by individual managers and submitted to the boss, or the boss writes them and gives them to the managers. These approaches can lead to (1) objectives not covering the most important RESULTS areas, (2) an activity objective on what is now being done by the manager rather than future oriented, and/or (3) objectives that are not effective for the total organization. The objectives may be correct in that they are well written in terms of measurement, time, cost, etc., but they may not be written on the *right* things. It is possible to be efficient in meeting objectives, but not effective from the organization's standpoint.

A brief description of how the MBO/R navigation and operation systems may be used will be given in this chapter. An in-depth discussion of each part will be found in following chapters.

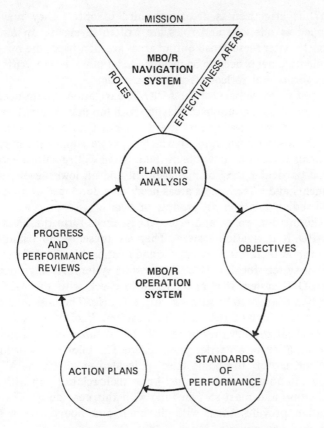

Fig. 7.1 MBO/R Navigation and Operation System.

MISSION, ROLES, AND EFFECTIVENESS AREAS

Mission—the purpose of the organization—needs to be clarified and made visible if it is not already visible. This is necessary in order that all managers in the organization can readily see how their efforts tie into and support it.

The role functions and relationships indicate how the mission will be carried out. In most cases roles need to be clarified immediately after the mission is developed. However, roles need to be reviewed after objectives are set because it may be necessary to change roles to achieve objectives.

While effectiveness areas are third in order, they may be developed as missions and roles are written to ensure an output approach. After these broad output areas are identified, the mission and role statements need to be reviewed to be sure they are written in output terms and reflect effectiveness areas.

The first three parts of the MBO/R navigation system need to be developed on a group basis starting with top management of the organization and moving downward. In practice, a point will be reached working downward at which separate supportive mission statements will not be possible as the mission will remain the same for that particular level of management and all lower levels. Role statements and effectiveness areas need to be developed at all levels for all individuals and all groups, or teams.

The mission, roles, and effectiveness areas form the basis for the MBO/R navigation system. They are presented in triangular form to show their interdependence and relationship. They form the guidance system for the MBO/R operation system. At any point in the MBO/R system it is appropriate to check with the MBO/R navigation triangle to be sure you are on course. The mission serves as the North Star of the navigation system. Each unit and each individual can see how they tie in with the organization. It is similar to the situation of a carrier pilot at sea. The pilot needs to know where the carrier, the home base, is located at all times. All individuals in an organization must know their relationship with the organization and must stay in tune with this constantly. The organization provides them with direction and boundaries within which they can operate.

MBO/R RECYCLING PROCESS

After the navigation system is set, the MBO/R operation system functions in a continuous recycling process. In the planning analysis, the groups and managers determine the priority areas that need attention. The group negotiation process is particularly important at this stage in order that there is group commitment to areas that need special attention and that will produce the most for the organization for the effort and resources put into them.

After the priority areas have been identified, the groups and managers will develop strategies for accomplishing them. This then provides the basis for writing specific results-oriented objectives. We emphasize these first two planning steps to ensure that objectives are written on the right things, the priority ones which will produce results.

Organizational objectives will be negotiated by units. Supportive individual objectives on both work items and personal development will be negotiated between bosses and subordinates and then checked out with peers. After objectives have been negotiated and action plans developed, roles should be checked to determine if it is necessary to renegotiate them as under MBO/R the organization needs to be organized around objectives. This may necessitate some changes in organization structure to facilitate the achievement of results.

The next step on the MBO/R operation model is standards of performance. These may be developed before or after action plans for objectives. When standards are inadequate, or unacceptable, it may be necessary to set objectives to correct the situation.

Action plans on each objective will determine how the traditional management functions of planning, organizing, controlling, and motivating are carried out. Action plans are necessary to validate each objective on understanding, desirability, achievability, and feasibility. This step ensures integration of existing systems into the MBO/R way of managing. It is also the way that each group and individual knows what is expected in order to achieve each organizational objective.

The action plans contain checkpoints or milestones when the group meets or checks with each other to determine whether they are on schedule. It provides the opportunity to make changes and possibly recycle into the planning analysis or objective setting steps if deemed appropriate to do so.

At this point there should be sufficient data to assess the progress of the group and individuals. Appropriate feedback systems are necessary to supply this data. The progress reviews should be held at least quarterly.

The performance review between boss and subordinate needs to be performed annually at a minimum. It provides information for the organization in the areas of manpower planning, salary and promotion and, for the individual, career and life planning.

From the progress reviews and/or performance reviews will

come the data to be used in the next planning analysis stage and the recycling process is underway. It is appropriate at this recycling point to check the guidance system of mission, roles, and effectiveness areas to be sure that what is being accomplished and planned is supportive of and within the mission and role boundaries.

USE OF MBO/R NAVIGATION AND OPERATION SYSTEMS

We see the chief use of the MBO/R navigation and operation systems to be diagnostic. Management is able to see the total picture of what steps have to take place in the complete MBO/R process. All of these do not have to be accomplished in the beginning, but eventually they will.

Considering the problems facing the organization on the management process, a manager may use this model to plan an orderly introduction of the MBO/R concept. It may start with developing a mission or validating an existing mission, role clarification, or objectives. If an organization is already into MBO/R, we suggest that management identify the problems being encountered and plug into this navigation and operation model where appropriate, making the minimum changes in the existing MBO/R system. Strategies may be developed to overcome existing problems gradually so that MBO/R is truly managing for RESULTS.

We emphasize that this MBO/R navigation system is not a panacea, but should be used and adapted to the needs, systems, and language of the organization. We developed it to help managers understand the concept and develop their own MBO/R system.

GROUP PROCESS

This navigation and operation model does not focus on the group negotiation process nor the boss-subordinate negotiation process. Both of these are essential to successful use of the model. The skills and competencies necessary for handling this process are covered in Chapter 16.

NOTES

1. We are indebted to Richard S. Underhill for his suggestions on the MBO/R navigation system.

MISSION—WHAT ARE
WE ALL ABOUT?

Mission, or purpose, is the base or foundation for the MBO/R concept. Even without considering MBO/R, it is necessary for effective planning, decision making, and budgeting. It has been called the number one fundamental decision to be made by top management. The mission is the North Star, the primary checkpoint, in the guidance system for managing an organization.

So often the mission is taken for granted and no one bothers to question it. It is a traumatic experience for a group to discover they cannot clearly define their mission and furthermore that there is considerable disagreement on what it is. We have also witnessed a group discovering that they had lost their mission. When reviewing their purpose for existence they found that everything listed was to meet *their* needs and the client was not even mentioned. After several proddings with "Why?", one member articulated the purpose that was given them by the parent organization when they were formed. It was "change in the client system—new behavior." This discovery brought about an in-depth exploration and self-examination of "what they were all about." A new understanding came as to why the group was beginning to fall apart and why the parent organization was becoming reluctant to continue supporting them. The North Star became visible again and they now had a basis for making decisions and clarifying their roles internally and with external groups.

MISSION IN RESULTS TERMS

Drucker writes that the mission is outside the organization.[1] It must be in terms of the customer or client. Their needs and wants (both satisfied and unsatisfied) have to be considered first and then what the organization is producing and can produce. To get this view, we suggest management put themselves in the position of the customer or client on the outside looking in at the organization.

Drucker writes that the customer is the foundation of a business and keeps it in existence.[2] Governmental and nonprofit organizations are in existence for clients and/or citizens.

An example of this occurred in a business organization—an oil company—that discovered its mission to be motorist satisfaction. Previously they had considered the dealer as their customer. After the new mission of motorist satisfaction was developed they realized the joint accountability with the dealer for meeting the needs of the motorist. This resulted in a whole new approach to working with the dealer.[3]

Another example, in the nonprofit sector, is the case of a youth services organization in state government that discovered their mission to be "delinquent youths and their families able to find personally satisfying ways of living in this society, which are free of illegal and/or self-destructive patterns of behavior." Previously they had considered their mission to be service to the juvenile court systems and juvenile homes. After the change and the acceptance of joint accountability on their mission, they started working differently with the courts and homes to accomplish results with the clients and their family.

The identification of RESULTS, or output, outside of the organization provides a basis for developing a way of effectively measuring when the organization is effective—when it is getting RESULTS. It will be easier to identify the times when there is success and when there is failure. This data will be helpful in making corrections, changes, and innovations to increase the success rate. In going this route the organization must be prepared in the short range for a high failure rate. This is not an increase in failures, but just an identification of what is and has been going on. They have been covered up by a lot of activities that people said could not be measured.

Quite often the only purpose given for the existence of a business organization is to make a profit. Drucker says this is meaningless. He further states that the first test of any business is not maximazation of profits but achievement of a sufficient profit to cover the risks of economic activity and thus avoid a loss. The purpose is more in the area of marketing and innovation.[4] Obviously profit is one of the reasons for existence of a business firm, but care needs to be exercised that profits not be used to avoid dealing with the real basic mission issue of "what business are we in?" Making a profit is an important measure of how successful the organization is in carrying out its mission or purpose, but it is not the only measure.

Etzioni emphasizes that the mission needs to be outside the organization to ensure that it is the master of the organization. If not, the mission can become the servant of the organization and be a means of self-perpetuation. This condition can gradually creep in when the needs of the organization increase and are perceived as more important than the mission.[5] MBO/R can greatly lessen the chance of this happening by keeping the mission visible at all times as the guidance system for developing objectives and making decisions.

In governmental organizations the mission has been written in terms of administering a law. Why was the law passed? What was the purpose of the law? A state division of motor vehicles found their mission to be traffic safety. The laws were a means, or an activity, to achieve the mission of traffic safety. After this discovery, their whole approach to legislation changed. They then made proposals to the legislature for new legislation rather than waiting for the legislators to tell them what to do. At the next session of the legislature they submitted a package of some fifty bills and failed on only three. A spokesman remarked that "we could have succeeded on those if we have done our homework." This is a change from a reactive position to a proactive one. There is much less chance of this happening with success if the organization is not focused on RESULTS. Management will have to examine the values of the organization in this process. How the organization values RESULTS and customer/client needs will have to be explored. This is where the values concepts discussed in Chapter 2 will come into play and influence the decision.

DEVELOPING A MISSION STATEMENT

We mentioned earlier that the mission of the organization is a fundamental decision that has to be made by top management. We think that it is essential that at least three levels of management, including the chief executive officer be involved in the initial development.

The mission statement developed by top management needs to be validated downward in the organization. This can be done by each unit at each level in the organization developing a mission statement supportive of the mission at the level immediately above. This should be carried downward to a point where the same mission statement can be written for horizontal units and from that point downward the mission statement will not change. In this way each unit and individual in the organization knows how they fit into the overall mission. There must be sufficient flexibility at the top level so that the organization's mission may be revised if the input from levels below indicate that this is in order.

We feel that these mission statements at all levels should be developed by working units or teams. This is essential because common outputs will be determined which in turn will determine priorities, roles and objectives. It may ultimately result in changes that will significantly affect functional areas. Consequently, understanding and commitment are necessary to the mission, or conflict will surface in other steps in the MBO/R navigation and operation model.

An example of how a change in mission can bring about changes in priorities and roles is the much-discussed Cunard Line mission. When operating under a mission that they were in the transportation business the emphasis was on engine speed and operation and stripped down furnishings and supplies. After changing their mission to the floating luxury hotel business, engine speed was no longer a priority. The important items became such things as, food, service, recreation, comfort, and furnishings.

Management at all levels will need some data in making their decisions on their mission. A thorough assessment of the internal environment and the external environment will have to be made. This is discussed in some detail in Chapter 11, Planning Analysis— Looking Ahead. There will be less need for data gathering at lower levels because it will be available to them from upper levels. The maximum data will be needed at the upper levels.

An individual unit within an organization may face the dilemma of not having and being unable to get a mission statement from the next upper level and/or for the organization as a whole. Rather than sitting powerless, we recommend that they identify their power and move ahead with the development of the mission for their unit. They, of course, will have to make assumptions about the mission above them as theirs must be supportive of it. They can then test their mission with management at the level above. More often than not this works, and the unit is able to progress with their movement into RESULTS management. This is more easily accomplished in semiautonomous units, such as regional offices, district offices, subsidiary operations, and individual plants. It has been our experience that when managers and units empower themselves in this manner their effectiveness increases, improved results are recognized both from above and horizontally, and rewards usually follow. Obviously there will be some failures and some reprimands. There is risk. Each manager and unit must be aware of it and decide how far they are willing to test the system.

CRITERIA FOR MISSION STATEMENT

A mission statement may be a sentence, a phrase, or a couple of phrases and/or sentences. It is broad and continuing in nature and does not change often. It may exist for years and never be fully accomplished. When the mission is accomplished, there is no longer a need for the organization unless it comes up with a new mission. An example of this is the National Foundation for Infantile Paralysis. The mission needs to be sufficiently broad and comprehensive to allow for growth of the organization. It can be too restrictive.

Some of the thought-provoking questions to be considered in developing a mission are (Note: Not all of these may be appropriate for each organization):

1. What business are we in?
2. Why are we in business?
3. What is our reason for existence?

4. What is our distinctiveness? our uniqueness?
5. How can we be more distinctive? unique?
6. What are we all about?
7. What are we doing?
8. What should we be doing?
9. When will our organization be performing acceptably?
10. What are the necessary areas of accomplishment?
11. What is our destination?
12. Where and what do we want to be five years from now? ten years?
13. What do we need to achieve? what RESULTS?

After the drafting of the mission statement, check it with the following: Is it understandable, brief, concise, broad, continuing in nature, self-contained, and stated in output (RESULTS) terms rather than activities (inputs)?[6]

To avoid the activity trap we have found it helpful to delete the traditional form of "To" followed by an action verb, e.g., To provide. . .; To serve. . .; To promote. . .; or To increase. . . . Typically, the action verb is followed by a "results" statement that is the accomplishment of task activity but *not necessarily* a RESULT that is outside of the organization which is defining its mission. Our approach uses this form: The mission of (organization) is (RESULT). The RESULT states the condition that will exist outside the organization after the group's action has been completed. It describes the desired RESULT without using the action verb or other verb forms.

For example, we would change:

The mission of the University of Richmond's Institute for Business and Community Development is to help individuals and organizations cope with a changing environment and self-renew for internal growth and development.

to

The mission of the University of Richmond's Institute for Business and Community Development is individuals and organizations able to cope with a changing environment and self-renew for internal growth and development.

To many this seems like a meaningless exercise that is just quibbling with words for no reason. "What difference does that make?" is the challenge. There is a significant difference in where the primary focus for commitment is. The first statement is an inward-looking view relative to the doing activity—to help. The second statement focuses on the RESULT that will occur outside of the organization because of what is done and is much more demanding in terms of accountability and responsibility. In the first case, many activities could be seen as helping and that's where the focus is. By changing the words and emphasis, accountability is focused on whether individuals and organizations are able to cope.

These principles on mission may also be applied to an individual's mission in life and could serve as a basis for career planning. This could be an appropriate way for boss and subordinate to start working the subordinate's personal objectives and career aspirations.

We think that it is apparent that considerable interaction will take place at all levels in the organization. It is important that management be aware of the necessity for groups to be able to handle the process of how they work together in making these decisions. In the early stages it is often necessary that external consulting help be used to improve this process so that there is an open, honest climate to fully utilize the resources of all involved.

NOTES

1. P. Drucker 1973. *Management*. New York. Harper & Row, p. 61.
2. *Op. cit.*, p. 61.
3. See "Grabbing Profits by the Roots" by Schleh in Chapter 5.
4. P. Drucker, *op. cit.*, pp. 64-65.
5. A. Etzioni 1964. *Modern organizations*. Englewood Cliffs, N.J.: Prentice-Hall, p. 10.
6. These questions were developed and expanded from a list developed by George Morrisey. G.L. Morrisey 1970. *Management by objectives and results*. Reading, Mass.: Addison-Wesley, pp. 20-32.

ROLE OUTPUTS AND RELATIONSHIPS

Roles will indicate the ways that an organization will carry out its mission. These will include both functions and relationships. The role functions will include the work that will be done, such as production, sales, accounting, personnel, engineering, training, etc. The role relationships will spell out the groups and/or individuals that the organization will serve or need in support of its mission. While these are important for an individual member, we feel they are more important for the effectiveness of the organization.

Roles establish the boundaries within which members and groups in the organization will operate. These boundaries will be for individual positions and subunits within the organization and for the whole organization insofar as other organizations are concerned. The establishment of roles empowers people to perform. By defining the boundaries within which they can perform, they can freely and totally use their competencies without being dependent on anyone for permission. This is the way that the concept of emPOWERment becomes operational. The interdependency that is necessary both within the organization and externally with other organizations is clearly established.

The importance of defining and clarifying roles early in the process cannot be overemphasized. If objectives are written before these boundaries are clear, there is considerable likelihood that some of the objectives developed will be in conflict. It is essential that each person and group know the work functions expected of them and what they can expect from other individuals and groups.

As roles are worked vertically and horizontally in the organization, gaps and overlaps usually are discovered. What are called personality conflicts are in reality mostly role conflicts. Either two individuals or groups are performing the same function and competing, or some work function is not being performed, thereby limiting the effectiveness of both individuals and the organization.

In entering an organization as external consultants, we often find that role clarification becomes evident as a first, or early, order of business. Members of the organization usually want these issues clarified and are grateful when help is given. Most people want to work together and be interdependent and thereby contribute to the organization.

When roles are not clear, the power in the organization is dissipated on them. The members disempower each other and their energy goes into fighting each other rather than into problem solving and creative thinking on how they can use their power together to move the organization forward and increase its effectiveness.

ROLE FUNCTIONS

Role functions are the major work efforts that an individual or group must perform to accomplish the basic purpose of the job. They need to be expressed in output (RESULT) terms rather than input (activity) terms. The typical form for role statements is a descriptive functional term(s) followed by the RESULT expected of that function. An example from a Personnel Department might be: *Employment and Placement*—Qualified or trainable people on the job. Some examples of role functions that might be included in departmental or unit responsibilities are sales, research, production, operations, accounting, engineering, and maintenance. There also need to be managerial role functions, such as policymaking, planning, resource management, staff development, and performance review.

It is essential that these role functions be clarified both on a group basis and an individual basis. This ensures that the effectiveness of each member will be viewed from an organizational viewpoint.

The following questions are suggested as a help in thinking through role functions:

1) What are we now doing? List.
2) Why do we do each of these things? (Keep asking "why" until an identifiable output is reached.)
3) Are these functions supportive of the mission?
4) What should we be doing in support of the mission? List.
5) Why should we do this? (Keep asking "why" until an identifiable output is identified.)
6) What is our distinctiveness? our uniqueness?
7) Is there a linkage of our functions with others?[1]

ROLE RELATIONSHIPS

In establishing role relationships, individuals and groups discover expectations that others have of them. Roles enable one to behave in a way that fulfills one's needs, provides satisfaction, and avoids punishment. They have certain characteristics and provide an individual or group a place in the system. They not only define relationships to others but also to the whole. They provide areas for appropriate behavior for individuals or groups and toward individuals and groups. They tend to clarify status, privileges and responsibilities, all of which contribute to a feeling of security and ease.[2]

As role relationships are clarified we think that it is important to establish psychological contracts (working agreements) on what each party is going to do for the other. This often leads to the development of standards of performance in which one person has to do certain things in a certain way by a certain time to meet the needs of another person in another job. These become standards for which the boss holds the person accountable. The word "contract" has considerable meaning in our society and using it from the psychological standpoint has a great impact on the individuals and groups involved. It may be appropriate that these contracts be in writing and become a basis for accountability. Managers and individuals need to confront each other when someone does not live up to the commitment made in the psychological contract. This is managing accountability which is necessary to making MBO/R work.

Some of the questions that might be helpful in developing role functions and relationships are:

1. Who are we serving?
2. What do we give each of them? (Product or service?) Why?
3. Who should we serve?
4. What should we give each of them? Why?
5. Who needs us? (Both inside and outside the organization.)
6. What do they need from us? What are the unsatisfied needs?
7. What expectations do others have of us? (Both inside and outside the organization.)
8. What and who are the market?
9. What should we be doing to accomplish our job?
10. What geographical area is served?
11. What is the financial (economic) commitment?
12. Is there a clear nonduplicating linkage to other individuals or groups? What are the areas of confusion and ambiguity?
13. What is the scope of the enterprise?[3]

Not all of these questions may be answered. They may stimulate thoughts in new areas not being handled now. The information developed in response to these questions along with similar data from working mission and effectiveness areas become part of the information base that is used in planning analysis as described in Chapter 11.

One suggested model for groups to use in clarifying role relationships will be found in Fig. 9.1. Each member of the group should complete the form independently and then share the data with the total group, preferably using chart paper posted on a wall fully visible to all. These role relationships will include boss, peers, subordinates, other departments or units, customers, clients, un-

Whom do I serve? (Product, service, etc. to indivdual and/or group)	What do I give them? (Product, service, etc. in what form, quality, quantity, and time)
1.	1. a) b) c) d) e)
2.	2. a) b) c) d) e)
etc.	etc.
Whom do I need to complete my task/operation? (individual and/or group)	What do I need from them? (Product, service, etc. in what form, quality, quantity, and time.)
1.	1. a) b) c) d) e)
2.	2. a) b) c) d) e)
etc.	etc.

Fig. 9.1 Clarifying Role Relationships

ions, and external groups such as other companies, wholesalers, re-
tailers, governmental agencies, legislative bodies, and volunteer
groups.

The group then has the necessary data to develop the
psychological contracts on how they are going to work together. This
can be total group, pairs or subgroups. It can be the basis for
developing a team or determining whether there is need for a team.
Where there is need for interdependent relationships, it will become
obvious. This form in Fig. 9.1 can be used to clarify role relation-

ships between two parties (boss-subordinate, peers, groups, etc.) by using only the righthand side, the "what" side. The data needs to be developed independently and then shared. A third party consultant may be necessary to help the process in the sharing, discussion, and contract development.

It has been our experience that members of an organization are unaware of role problems. Or at least they have been unable, or unwilling, to articulate them. Many times the problems that are identified in the organization are in reality only symptoms of role conflicts caused by unclear boundaries between individuals and/or groups. Until these are clarified and the members empower each other, they will expend their energy on symptoms and little lasting progress will be made. The role expectations between boss and subordinate have been surveyed by numerous consultants. It has consistently shown a 25 percent discrepancy between how the boss sees a subordinate's job and how the subordinate sees it. As long as this discrepancy exists, conflicts can be expected. This will be especially true when the boss is evaluating the subordinates on one set of expectations and subordinates are evaluating their performance on another set. It is imperative that a psychological contract be negotiated between boss and subordinates before the evaluation period in order that there is a match of expectations.

In Fig. 9.2 is another form that might be helpful in role negotiation. It can be used the same way as suggested for the form in Fig. 9.1 for a group, subgroup, or pairs.

Message From: _____ To: _____

---

1. If you were to do the following things *more* or *better*, it would help me to increase my own effectiveness.

2. If you were to do the following things *less*, or where to *stop* doing them, it would help me to increase my own effectiveness.

3. The following things which you have been doing help to increase my effectiveness, and I hope you will continue to do them.

Fig. 9.2 Issue diagnosis.[4]

PROCEDURE FOR DEVELOPING ROLES

Roles spell out how the mission will be carried out. Consequently, roles must be developed after the mission statement. There often is confusion between mission statements and role statements. Therefore they should be differentiated and developed separately. After both are developed, they are usually integrated into one statement of mission and roles with the mission being a preamble, establishing the "What," followed by several role statements defining the means by which that mission will be accomplished.

Role statements need to be developed at *all* levels in the organization. Each level's roles will be supportive of those at the level immediately above. As they are developed vertically, they necessarily have to be worked horizontally so that accountability is clear upward, downward, and laterally. The result will be statements both for groups and for individuals. At the individual level they may replace the customary job description.

In developing role statements, especially at the top management level, values will have to be examined. The philosophy or code of ethics of the organization will have to be articulated. The attitude of the management of a business organization toward stockholders, employees and unions, customers or clients, government, community, and society as a whole should be explored. Governmental organizations will be concerned with citizens, legislature, business organizations, and other governmental units. Other organizations will be concerned with their members, clients, community, and government. The values of the organization will be reflected in its role statements. Some organizations develop creeds or codes of ethics, which are supportive. This may be appropriate, but it must be for more than show or public relations to be of any value operationally. Top management must behave in line with this code and therefore become a guide for behavior throughout the organization.

As role statements are developed at all levels in the organization, it is imperative that there be a high level of vertical and horizontal integration to ensure commitment. The process of a group working together on roles will cause the surfacing of feelings, attitudes, and behaviors which must be recognized and dealt with. It may be traumatic for an individual or unit to realize that they are duplicating a function and that they are not needed. The group may also discover that certain necessary functions are not being performed. Some members and groups may have to give up "turf" and change what they are doing. This reality may cause fear and a fight for survival which may surface as conflict. Managers and groups need to have the skill to manage this conflict. If they are unable to handle conflict, a consultant may be used to facilitate resolution and to develop conflict management skills within the group.

NOTES

1. These questions were developed and expanded from a list developed by George Morrisey. G. L. Morrisey 1970. *Management by objectives and results.* Reading, Mass.: Addison-Wesley, pp. 20-22.

2. D. Nylen, J.R. Mitchell, and A. Stout 1967. *Handbook of staff development and human relations training.* Washington, D.C. National Training Laboratories, p. 60.

3. Morrisey, *op. cit.*, pp. 20-32. Developed from a list by George Morrisey.

4. R. Harrison 1974. Role negotiation: a tough-minded approach to team development. In M. L. Berger and R. S. Berger (eds.), *Group Training Techniques.* New York: Wiley, p. 90.

FOCUSING ON EFFECTIVENESS

The third item in the MBO/R navigation system is effectiveness areas (EA). This is similar to key results areas used by some authors and consultants. Sometimes the terms are used interchangeably.

W.J. Reddin defines effectiveness areas in the article which follows in this chapter as "the output requirements of a job." The development of effectiveness areas for each job and each unit is essential in identifying RESULTS (outputs) desired. Without these, it is easy to be concerned with activities and tasks only and the RESULTS orientation necessary for success of the MBO/R concept will be missing.

As the third item in the MBO/R navigation system it is vital to the development of mission and role statements in output terms. Consequently, after the EAs are developed for a position or unit, the mission and roles need to be checked to be sure they are written in output terms and there is no conflict among the three. Hence a triangle is used in the MBO/R navigation model in Chapter 7 to show the connection.

We think that effectiveness is an essential concept of the MBO/R process. A manager or unit is effective to the extent that he, or they, are able to achieve the output or performance requirements of that position. Effectiveness areas are broad; written in two to four words; contain no verbs, dates, standards of measurement, nor directional indicators such as increase and reduce. Examples of effectiveness areas are in the following article by W.J. Reddin.

They are limited to 5 to 7 for each position and cover 100 percent of the job.

Following are a few questions and suggestions to help in identifying and developing effectiveness areas:

1. Where does asking "Why?" lead?
2. What is our unique contribution?
3. What is the biggest thing which could go wrong?
4. Why was our position created?
5. What do we do or could we do that subordinates do not because:
   a. They don't have the ability or experience
   b. They don't have the time
   c. They don't have the information.
6. Where is our recognizable output? (An activity at a higher organizational level may be a RESULT at a lower level.)
7. Unit effectiveness areas
   a. By what criteria would we decide our team is performing well?
   b. What is the necessary area of accomplishment?
   c. Against what criteria should the performance of our team be measured?
   d. Note against each area how its attainment could be measured accurately.[1]

EFFECTIVENESS MEASUREMENT CRITERIA (EMC)

Effectiveness areas provide the framework for the development of specific measurement indicators of performance. As the next step in the process effectiveness measurement criteria[2] should be developed under each EA. Examples of EMCs are: (1) if sales in an EA, the EMCs might be area, product, and customer or the EMCs might be by individual products or product groups; (2) if safety is an EA, the EMCs might be lost time accidents, medical treatment accidents, and inspections; (3) training (EA) might have EMCs technical, management, and organization development; and (4) accounts receivable (EA) might have EMCs billing, collections, and errors. The number of EMCs under an EA may be from two to six, or possibly more.

After the effectiveness measurement criteria have been developed under each effectiveness area, a manager or unit is in a position to write objectives and standards of performance for those situations which have the greatest potential or highest priority.

For a more thorough in-depth discussion of the effectiveness areas concept, we recommend reading *Effective management by objectives* by W. J. Reddin.[3] We consider it a helpful text in working with the MBO/R concept.

NOTES

1. These were developed and expanded from a list by W. J. Reddin. W. J. Reddin 1971. *Effective management by objectives.* New York: McGraw-Hill, p. 67.
2. These are called effectiveness standards by W. J. Reddin.
3. Reddin, *op. cit.* pp. 23-77.

EFFECTIVE MANAGEMENT JOB DESCRIPTIONS

W.J. REDDIN

There is only one realistic and unambiguous definition of managerial effectiveness: effectiveness is the extent to which a manager achieves the output requirements of his position. When it is seen this way, the concept of managerial effectiveness becomes the central issue in management. It is the manager's job to be effective. It is his only job. Once this definition is accepted and understood it can lead directly to changes in personnel policy, major changes in management development practices and in the philosophy underlying management by objectives (MBO).

Reprinted with permission of W. J. Reddin, W. J. Reddin and Associates, New Brunswick, Canada.

To understand what managerial effectiveness is, it is necessary to distinguish sharply among the three terms *managerial effectiveness, apparent effectiveness,* and *personal effectiveness.*

Managerial effectiveness: It is not an aspect of personality. It is not something a manager has. To see it this way is nothing more or less than a return to the now discarded trait theory of leadership, which suggested that more effective leaders have special qualities not possessed by less effective leaders. Effectiveness is best seen as something a manager produces from a situation by managing it appropriately. In current terminology it represents output, not input. The manager must think in terms of performance, not personality. It is not so much what a manager does, but what he achieves. The following is an extreme example:

A manager's true worth to his company may sometimes be measured by the amount of time he could remain dead in his office without anyone noticing. The longer the time, the more likely it is that he makes long-run policy decisions rather than short-run administrative decisions. The key decisions in a company are long run and may refer to market entry, new-product introduction, new-plant location, or key man appointments. The person making these decisions should not get involved as can happen with short-run issues. If he does, he has not decided on the output measures of his job, nor has he the skill or opportunity to create conditions where only policy issues reach him.

Some managers have narrow views of their jobs. What they do they may do well, but they leave an enormous amount undone. Some managers let the in-basket define the nature of their potential contribution and the clock its limit. One manager might view his contribution as simply that of managing a going concern and keeping it on an even keel, while another might see the same job as having large components of subordinate development and creative problem solving in it. Still another might see his position primarily as a linking pin connecting with other parts of the firm, and thus might take a wider view of his responsibility.

Apparent effectivess: It is difficult, if not impossible, to judge managerial effectiveness by observation of behavior alone. The behavior must be evaluated in terms of whether or not it is appropriate to the output requirements of the job. For example, the following qualities, while important in some jobs, may in others be irrelevant to effectiveness: Usually is on time, answers promptly, makes quick decisions, is good at public relations, is good writer.

These qualities usually give an air of apparent effectiveness in whatever context they may appear. But apparent effectiveness may or may not lead to managerial effectiveness. For example, consider the case of Charles Smith, an independent consultant with four employees. He was the first one in and last one out each day. He virtually ran everything and ran everywhere. In a business which usually makes low demands for immediate decisions, he always made them on the spot. "Do it now" was his catch phrase. He was very intelligent, active, optimistic, aggressive, and his job input was enormous. His staff turnover, however, was 100 percent in one year, and he sometimes signed contracts which he had no possibility of meeting. If his business failed, the casual observer might well say, "It wasn't because of Charlie," thus showing the confusion that exists over the important differences between apparent effectiveness and managerial effectiveness.

Conventional job descriptions often lead to an emphasis on what could be called *managerial efficiency:* the ratio of output to input. The problem is that if both input and output are low, efficiency could still be 100 percent. In fact, a manager or department could easily be 100 percent efficient and zero percent effective. The efficient manager is easily identified. He prefers to:

	do things right	rather than	do right things,
	solve problems	rather than	produce creative alternatives;
	safeguard resources	rather than	optimize resource utilization;
and	discharge duties	rather than	obtain results.

Conventional job descriptions lead to the apparent effectiveness of the behavior as listed in the left column; a job effectiveness description which emphasized managerial effectiveness would lead to performance as listed in the column on the right.

Conventional job descriptions and management audits usually focus on the internal efficiency of an organizational system rather than on its external effectiveness or its outputs. It would be a simple matter to increase internal efficiency sharply and to decrease external effectiveness just as sharply. Paperwork usually is quite unrelated to effectiveness.

The distinction between managerial effectiveness and apparent effectiveness can be further illustrated by what really happens when a "steamroller" manager brings what appears to be chaos to an organization but the situation clearly begins to improve. Unless outputs are the focus of attention, the result can be serious distortion about what is really going on.

Personal effectiveness: Poorly defined job outputs can also lead to what might be called personal effectiveness: that is, the satisfying of personal objectives rather than the objectives of the organization. This is particularly likely to occur with ambitious men in an organization having only a few closely defined management output measures. Meetings with these men are riddled with hidden agendas, which operate below the surface and lead to poor decision making. To illustrate: in a three-day meeting to set corporate objectives for a Toronto consumer goods firm, one of the four vice-presidents in attendance initiated a series of proposals for reorganization and argued for them with great force.

While all had some merit, it became clear, as he described them, that most would not lead to greatly improved team effectiveness. Other team members saw quickly that all these proposals were aimed, to some extent unconsciously, at improving the vice-president's power and prestige. This issue was confronted for several hours and the team members, many of whom had previously had intentions similar to those of the vice-president, finally decided to turn their attention away from improving their personal effectiveness to improving their managerial effectiveness and, therefore, their total team effectiveness. The top management structure was modified but in keeping with market, consumer, competitive, and organizational needs; not with personal needs.

There is nothing wrong with either personal effectiveness or apparent effectiveness. We all like to make it in our own terms and we all like to appear effective. The problem arises only when either condition is confused with managerial effectiveness. In a well-designed firm, all three kinds of effectiveness could occur simultaneously for a particular manager. This would mean that a manager who is in fact effective looks as if he is (apparent effectiveness), and is rewarded for it (personal effectiveness).

THE DEADLY SIN OF INPUTS

The first step in helping managers to be more effective is to help them see their job in output terms. To keep the concept of effectiveness in mind, we can refer to these outputs as *effectiveness areas*, but they can have a variety of other names. The problem is that too many jobs are described in terms of inputs, not outputs: in terms of *input areas* and not in terms of *effectiveness areas.*

The source of much of the problem which surrounds effectiveness is found in the way job descriptions are written. Lengthy job descriptions or crash programs to write or update them usually have little actual usefulness. As C. Northcote Parkinson has pointed out, the last act of a dying organization is to issue a revised and greatly enlarged rule book. This observation may hold as well for crash programs to write job descriptions.

Many, if not most, managerial jobs are defined in terms of their input and behavior requirements by such phrases as: *he administers . . . . he maintains . . . . he organizes . . . . he plans . . . .* and *he schedules.* Naturally enough, managers never refer to job descriptions like these; once made, they are not very useful as an operating guide. They are often proposed initially by those who want to use a seemingly scientific technique to justify a widespread change in salary differentials or a change in the organization structure. They are often a negative influence, as they focus on input and behavior, the less important aspect of the manager's job.

The most common error in writing effectiveness areas is in producing input areas instead. An input area is an incorrect statement of an effectiveness area which is based on activities or inputs rather than results or outputs.

One director of agricultural extension working with a staff of about forty initially established the following effectiveness areas: (1) filling of staff positions adequately, (2) competence of staff, (3) turnover of professional staff, (4) organizing and developing an extension program, (5) promoting activity in farm youth clubs, (6) conducting studies and preparing reports (7) supervising loan grants to farmers. (These areas were covered in his first attempt).

After becoming acquainted with the managerial effectiveness concept, and particularly with methods of establishing effectiveness areas, he decided that this first attempt needed improvements. In particular, he saw that he was taking no responsibility for change, and that he was focusing on inputs, not outputs. His proposed effectiveness areas indicated a low-level bureaucratic view of his job. Like many of those employed by government, he greatly over-emphasized staffing, programs, and report writing. All of these are important, of course, but they do not relate directly to the basic function of the position.

The director made a second attempt at setting his effectiveness areas, concentrating this time on the areas of: (8) net farm income, (9) percentage of commercial farmers, (10) high-value crop acreage, and (11) the average number of livestock.

This second attempt very clearly focuses on an end result on output, not input. In discussion, however, this director found that to some extent he had gone too far the other way. He could not make "net farm income" an effectiveness area because so many factors affected it over which he had no control, including such things as government policy and farm board decisions. His third attempt was somewhere between the first and second attempts.

In his third attempt he became involved with the areas of: (12) average farm acreage, (13) securing farm loans, (14) high-value crop acreage, (15) average number of livestock, and (16) farmer knowledge.

Areas 10 (high-value crop acreage) and 11 (average number of livestock) remain. Area 8 (net farm income) was removed. Two of the director's major resources used to help increase net farm income were loans to farmers and educational staff, programs, and facilities. The director decided to make these into effectiveness areas, largely to replace "net farm income." His final areas were focused on ends, not means: on what he had to achieve, not what he did. The objective associated with all of these effectiveness areas were easily measurable and all were clearly output, not input.

In a letter to the author, the director wrote:

Number 1 was my first attempt at setting these down. Number 2 presented my first change. Number 3 is what I thought was a refinement on the second. I am still not completely satisfied with these and I will now discuss these at some length with my superior in order to arrive at what we both feel is the best set of effectiveness areas for my position. The problem that I faced initially in preparing them was that I am in a position of directing a number of program areas, and a lot of the decisions I make are with reference to staffing, budgeting, personnel, and additions to programs. This led me to lose sight of what I was actually supposed to accomplish.

Too many attempts to set effectiveness areas fall into one of the two traps illustrated by this manager's first and second attempts. Either they focus on inputs and turn managers into bureaucrats, or they deal with uncontrollable outputs and so become predictions, dreams, or simply part of another manager's job.

THE TRAINING OFFICER

While many initial attempts to set effectiveness areas turn out instead to be a list of activities, many attempts can go in the other direction: everyone then appears to think he is heading a profit center. Of any proposed effectiveness area the question should be asked, "Why is this being done?" or "Why is this important?" For example, a training manager might go through this kind of process. He is first asked what his most important area is. To which he might reply: "To design a management development program." When asked "Why?" he replies, "To put on courses for managers." When again asked "Why?" he replies, "To increase managerial skill in problem solving." when again asked "Why?" he replies, "To improve the quality of managerial decisions." To yet another "Why?" he replies, "To improve profit performance." The correct area for this training manager would probably be "to increase managerial skill in problem solving." It cannot be "to improve the quality of managerial decisions" or "to improve profit performance," as these are both influenced by many factors over which the training manager has no control. He has no authority. On the other hand, the areas cannot be simply "program design" or "putting on courses," which are clearly inputs. The sole objective of industrial training is to change behavior. The effectiveness areas and the objectives of a training manager must reflect this.

Most inputs can be converted to outputs if the position is needed at all. Some examples of inputs converted to outputs are the following: *maintain machines* to *machine availability; coach subordinates* to *subordinate effectiveness; teach PERT* to *PERT usage; church attendance* to *Christian values;* and *farmer education* to *high-value crop acreages.* One should beware of such areas as communication, relationships, liaison, coordination, and staffing: these areas usually suggest inputs.

FROM INPUTS TO OUTPUTS

The following are actual examples of improved effectiveness areas, showing both first and second attempts at establishing them. The first attempt was most-often produced as private work without consultation. The second attempt shows how these first attempts were improved after a small group discussion. Such before-after changes as these are typical. They demonstrate what an imperfect view many, or even most, managers have of their jobs, and how easy it is to change this view, given the appropriate method and conditions. None of the second attempts is claimed to be perfect for the job in question, and in any case this would be impossible to determine without much more information. The point being made is that the second attempt clearly is better than the first.

CHAIRMAN OF THE BOARD

A full-time chairman of the board of a 6000-employee company produced these two sets of effectiveness areas:

First attempt: (1) improve value of board, (2) ensure good executive meetings, (3) provide useful counsel to company officers, (4) maintain effective remuneration and personnel policies for senior executives, (5) develop good high-level corporate image and public relations, and (6) initiate sound long-range planning.

Second attempt: (7) board decision quality, (8) national corporate image, and (9) corporate strategy.

The realization that the second set of areas was really his job led this chairman of the board to make many changes, particularly in his time allocation. He saw that number 1 (improve value of board) and number 2 (ensure good executive meetings) could be replaced by number 7 (board decision quality), that 3 (provide useful counsel to company officers) was meddling, and that 4 (maintain effective remuneration and personnel policies for senior executives) should be given to the president, to whom 5 (develop good high-level corporate image and public relations) was his job, but on a national scale, as expressed in 8 (national corporate image), and that 6 (initiate sound long-range planning) was best replaced by 9 (corporate strategy).

PRESIDENT OF 5000-EMPLOYEE FOOD PROCESSOR

The president of a 5000-employee food processor initially produced a set of thirteen effectiveness areas.

First attempt: (1) profitability; (2) planning; (3) top team quality; (4) profit growth; (5) reputation growth; (6) growth momentum; (7) trade relations; (8) industry relations; (9) government relations; (10) board and employee relations; (11) capital employment; (12) return on investment; and (13) management succession plan.

Second attempt: (14) profitability, (15) planning, (16) reputation in industry, (17) company climate, and (18) customer-top management relations.

This company president decided to retain number 1 (profitability) and number 2 (planning) as numbers 14 (profitability) and 15 (planning). Area 3 (top team quality) he identified as a common area; 4 (profit growth) could be included as a subobjective of 14 (profitability) by using a longer time span; 5 (reputation growth) was changed to 16 (reputation in industry)—he kept this as he was a marketing-oriented president who spent much of his time on customer and industry visits; 6 (growth momentum) moved to 14 (profitability); 7 (trade relations) moved to part of 16 (reputation in industry); and 8 (industry relations) became more specific as 18 (customer-top management relations). Number 9 (government relations) was identified as the executive vice-president's area exclusively; 10 (board and employee relations) he changed to 17 (company climate); 11 (capital employment) and 12 (return on investment) were given to the vice-president of finance; and 13 (management succession plan) was seen as an area belonging to the vice-president of personnel.

JOB OUTPUTS ARE ALWAYS MEASURABLE

If a so-called effectiveness area or objective is not measurable, we can forget it, because no one will know anyway. The sternest but necessary test of effectiveness areas and objectives is measurability. The rule is "if you cannot measure it, forget it."

In the lefthand column of the following discussion is a list of qualitative objectives which are used as an illustration in one popular MBO book to suggest that such qualitative objectives must sometimes be used. This is incorrect. To illustrate, in the righthand column are this author's conversions to show that such qualitative objectives are usually unnecessary.

Actual suggested qualitative objectives in standard MBO book	Conversion to illustrate the qualitative objectives are usually found to be activities.
	By asking the purpose of the activities, the quantitative objectives are derived.
Conduct monthly management development sessions for superintendents in techniques of standard cost program.	Have 50 percent of superintendents using standard cost programming techniques on at least two projects EO JUL 1974.
Prepare a program for patent productions.	Have no patent loopholes in our patents discovered by our own staff, independent agents, or competitors during 1974.
Prepare and distribute an internal public relations manual.	Obtain an average of 75 percent unaided recall by all nonmanagerial employees of 50 percent of the key corporate activities or accomplishments of the prior month for each month during 1975.

Improve statistical reports to reduce time lag between production and publication dates.	Without decreasing usable content, reduce by an average of four days the time to distribute the following reports by the end of SEPT 1974.
Prepare quality control manual for supervisors.	Eighty-five percent of first-line supervisors to know eight of the ten key points in company quality control practice by the end of DEC 1974.
Improve appearance, packaging, and design of products.	For each item in product line, design a package which will receive more consumer jury votes than any competing product by the end of NOV 1974.
Undertake to ally research efforts more closely with production needs.	Have at least 80 percent of proposals to production manager accepted during 1974.

It is true that most of these conversions from inputs to outputs involve a broader view of one's job, a greater responsibility for the staff function, and a higher cost of measurement.

EFFECTIVENESS AREAS—KNOWLEDGE WORKERS

It is a popular myth that the effectiveness of many knowledge workers cannot be measured. But look at this set of effectiveness areas, disarmingly simple, all of which are capable of measurement if the associated objectives are worded correctly:

Consulted in area of competence

Advice accepted

Advice acceptance leads to improvement

The first area, *consulted in area of competence,* obliges the knowledge worker, not the manager, to see that the knowledge worker is consulted. Too many knowledge workers, like some university professors, see themselves as information reservoirs with no responsibility to provide a "tapping" facility; and usually this is sorely needed. Knowledge workers, more than managers, have the opportunity to develop a relationship so that their advice is sought when appropriate. Industry has no place for the knowledge worker who does not himself create consultative conditions.

The second area, *advice accepted,* reflects that it is too easy to give advice that is not accepted. The knowledge worker must be evaluated on his effectiveness in giving advice a line manager sees he can use. The final area is *advice acceptance leads to improvement.* As it is too easy to give advice not accepted, it is also too easy to give advice that leads to "a poorer situation developing." The knowledge worker has a responsibility for the success of his advice. Personal competence is not listed as an effectiveness area. It is an input. In any case, if the knowledge worker was not competent, his advice would not lead to improvement.

While the measurement problem usually can be solved with imagination, the *cost of measurement* problem may remain. To measure the impact of a training course on behavior necessitates at least many telephone calls or questionnaires, and preferably a field survey. The outputs of a public relations position are hard to measure without a formal survey of some kind. In these cases one has to ask whether the function is important enough to have even a rough measurement of its effectiveness. If not, then eliminate the function. If so, then allocate 10 percent of the total appropriate budget to measurement. There is too much conventional wisdom that a particular activity is a "good thing." Measurement is the only way to test it.

It is difficult for some managers to accept the philosophy that "if you cannot measure it, forget it, because no one will know anyway." Accurate measurement is central to good management. Some managers initially see their job as having vague, pervasive, and very long-term effects and claim that it is impossible to measure their performance by normal methods. If such a manager also says that he understands what managerial effectiveness really means, then he: (1) is in a position that is not needed, (2) has no authority to do his job, or (3) is avoiding responsibility.

As a simple example, a good relationship is often proposed as an effectiveness area. This is not measurable except by highly subjective methods. A sales manager who once proposed this area said later that it was not only nonmeasurable but it was an input as well; he saw that his effectiveness in this area could be equally well measured by short- and long-term sales.

IS THERE A JOB AT ALL?

If two people are responsible for the same things, one of them is not needed. Major problems occur in such areas as delegation and planning when a manager sees his effectiveness areas as being simply the sum of all his subordinates' effectiveness areas.

Some superiors who misunderstand their jobs believe that, in essence, it is to make sure their subordinates do what they are supposed to do. This view, if taken to its natural conclusion, means that the sole function of all levels of management is to make sure that the workers get on with it. This clearly is incorrect and it would mean that all levels of management existed to see that the workers at the very lowest level worked. While it may be true in some technologies, it is not true in many. We simply cannot say that a superior's job is always well represented simply by a collection of his subordinates' effectiveness areas, or their objectives.

A Canadian vice-president supervised four managers of profit centers. He knew he had difficulty in determining his own effectiveness areas; one area could not be profit, because this was an area of each of his subordinates. He had no resources such as capital to allocate among them; in fact, he did not have a job. At a meeting held for this unit it became clear he had no job. The team recommended that, as a unit, it be dissolved. The four profit centers became attached to other parts of the organization and the vice-president fully assumed another role which he had previously filled only nominally.

It is clear that for every position, effectiveness areas must be identifiable. What typically happens is that in his first attempt, the manager accepts the fact that all his effectiveness areas are really those of his subordinates. While apparently left with nothing to do, he knows he is filling a useful role. With further thought he comes to see his unique contribution only dimly perceived before. With his real job identified, he gets on with it rather than with the jobs of his subordinates.

PERSONNEL MANAGER

One personnel manager listed his effectiveness areas as: training, wage and salary administration, employment (staffing), safety and security, and industrial relations. He was then asked to draw himself and his subordinates as an organization chart and to identify all the effectiveness areas, starting with those of subordinates, and not to duplicate any. The result is shown in Exhibit One. He ran out of effectiveness areas before he got to his own position. This meant that he saw his position as having no unique responsibilities. His job, as he had defined it, was either doing his subordinates' work or making sure they did it. This was a narrow definition of his responsibility. He could see his job in broader terms than that and, surely, he has more to contribute.

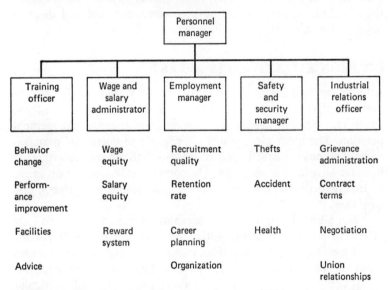

Exhibit One What is the job of the personnel manager? (When your subordinates share all your effectiveness areas, what are you left with?)

He was asked these questions: What is your unique contribution? What is the biggest thing which could go wrong? What do you or could you do that the managers do not because: (1) they do not have the ability or experience? (2) they do not have the time? or (3) they do not have the information? Why was your position created?

This personnel manager came to see that his unique contribution was in the areas of: personnel policy, working conditions, organizational development, and managerial effectiveness. He could not accept full responsibility for all of these areas but was responsible, as any staff person, for giving acceptable advice which would prove correct. When we compare his first set of effectiveness areas to his revised set, they show a greatly enlarged view of the job, and a preparedness to allow subordinates to get on with it.

As he had fairly experienced subordinates, he could allow them to work with full authority in their respective positions. If he lost a position in his structure or a key subordinate, he might have to take the effectiveness areas of the position concerned and add them to his own for a while.

COMMON EFFECTIVENESS AREAS

All management positions, no matter how different, do have some common effectiveness areas. Common effectiveness areas are those which may be, and usually are, associated with every management position. The other areas which are specific to particular management positions are called specific areas—all that have been referred to so far have been of this type. The common effectiveness areas are called: subordinate, innovative, project, development, systems, and coworker.

Not all of the common effectiveness areas meet the stern tests of output and completely objective measurement suggested for the specific effectiveness areas. This is because common effectiveness areas are, by their very nature, designed simply to ensure organizational continuity rather than to achieve the outputs of particular positions.

SUBORDINATE EFFECTIVENESS AREA

Every management position having positions subordinate to it needs to have subordinate effectiveness as an effectiveness area. This effectiveness area serves to focus sharply on the true relationship needed between the supervisor and his subordinate.

An associated objective could be worded like this: "Each subordinate is to establish by 15 August 1971 measurable objectives which are agreed to by those concerned, and which align horizontally and vertically." Such an objective substitutes for customary objectives concerning motivation, control, relationships, and delegation, which do not get to the heart of the matter: *effectiveness.*

Unnecessary emphasis is sometimes used in the wording of objectives concerning subordinates: "To ensure that subordinates will achieve . . . ." "To motivate subordinates to achieve . . . ." These phrases sound powerful and dynamic, but add nothing.

INNOVATIVE EFFECTIVENESS AREA

The innovative effectiveness area refers to doing something new on one's own initiative. It does not refer to doing things better or to implementing innovations which others propose. The mere existence of this as a common effectiveness area results in annual questioning of "the way we are doing things now." Associated objectives might concern proposals or implementation: "Propose X new," "Introduce X new." If proposing new products is not normally part of one's job, the following objective might apply: "During 1974 propose five new products to the product committee, each with a four-year sales potential of $X and have one accepted for trial testing." This objective may be somewhat grand for a manager who does not have innovation as his full-time job. More realistic objectives may relate to innovations in methods or procedure.

PROJECT EFFECTIVENESS AREA

Another common effectiveness area is project effectiveness. Projects concern activities which are not a normal part of the job and are not innovations to the existing job. They most usually arise from an assignment from the manager's superior. Its associated objectives refer to projects which are usually of a "one-shot" nature. They may refer to such things as: project committee membership, conversion of paper files to microfilm, appraisal of any system, redesign of any system, initiation of any system, conducting special investigations, and temporary assignment to other departments.

Such objectives usually refer to such things as feasibility studies and trial applications—untested, new systems. The objectives may form the basis of project team problem solving and are usually self-cancelling once the objective is achieved. Project objectives can have a lower priority than others, and of course they may vary widely from year to year.

DEVELOPMENT EFFECTIVENESS AREA

The term *development effectiveness area* refers to that area involved with preparing to meet the objectives of the position. This may include: human skills acquisition, technical skill acquisition, conceptual skill acquisition, and work habit modification. There may be only one single objective in a particular year which could be worded "Prepare myself during 1974 to be able to meet my objectives now established and those which will probably be established during the next X years."

The associated activities could include: making a time budget, reading specific management books, obtaining practice in the use of PERT diagrams for objectives, participating in seminars, visiting and attending conferences.

All managers would wish to set at least one objective in this area each year. If they do not, it is unlikely that they are improving their overall capacity at the rate they are capable of doing. On the other hand, overemphasis on this kind of thing simply indicates a man who hasn't got a job. He develops himself and not the business.

Many of these developmental objectives have a strong flavor of input rather than output, but should be made output-oriented when possible. For instance, concerning training, don't say "attend a five-day PERT network seminar," but "be able to use PERT for at least two of my objectives," or better, "use PERT for at least two of my objectives."

SYSTEMS EFFECTIVENESS AREA

A manager is part of the system. If the system does not work, the achievement or lack of achievement of his objectives is inconsequential. Clearly, all managers have a responsibility to respond to the superstructure of the system in which their position is embedded. Some managers carry it too far and believe that an ideal manager in all circumstances is the bureaucrat who is interested first in maintaining the system. On the other hand, the single-minded pursuit of an objective while not also considering the firm as a system means only that a manager has learned the name of the game, not the spirit of it.

Systems effectiveness is needed as a common effectiveness area. It relates to a manager's responsibility to see that his position and unit fits well into the broader scheme of budgets and procedures. A budget is a device for making an organization work as designed; in the same way, so are standard operating procedures. An associated objective might be worded: "to maintain the company budget, procedural, and administrative control systems."

Budget should not be included, of course, if the manager has no budget responsibility, nor if he is also a revenue center when a "margin" or "cost per dollar received" objective can be used instead, nor if the budget is so constructed as to have only one to three key items, in which case it is often a good idea to express the objectives in terms of these instead of as a common effectiveness area.

CO-WORKER EFFECTIVENESS AREA

Co-worker effectiveness is a common effectiveness area only for those who have co-workers. The common area exists to emphasize the role of the manager as an external representative of his department. It gives recognition to the essential linking needed for a firm's subparts if organizational effectiveness is to be achieved.

An associated objective might be worded "in the opinion of each co-worker, to have done nothing to inhibit his managerial effectiveness." Some managers prefer to word this positively as: "in the opinion of each co-worker, to have aided him in achieving his managerial effectiveness." While the measurement method is a trifle subjective, the method itself is clear—you ask them.

Some managers shy away from this common effectiveness area with a variety of excuses. It is sometimes because they have been trained too well to look upward and downward in the organization, and not across.

DO ALL APPLY?

Do all the common effectiveness areas apply to all management positions? The rule is "when in doubt, try to make them apply." One MBO adviser with a firm which had a low rate of new-product launches and low creativity suggested initially that the innovative effectiveness area could not generally apply. He was trapped by the firm he was in. The very reason it appeared to be difficult naturally suggested its use there. If a common area is seen not to apply, it is best to take a close look at the reasons given. They may be obvious and correct. On the other hand, they may be neither. When possible, then, all managers should attempt to apply all the common areas to their positions.

DO EFFECTIVENESS AREAS COVER THE WHOLE JOB?

One of the more interesting differences of approach of writers of MBO books is in the percentage of the job that they believe should be covered by effectiveness areas. I believe that effectiveness areas, and therefore objectives, must cover 100 percent of the job. To some extent this is facilitated by the "common areas" concept.

HOW TO SELECT EFFECTIVENESS AREAS

Here is a list of simple questions for a manager to ask himself, and then be able to develop an initial list of effectiveness areas for his position to test on his superior and his co-workers. There is much overlap in the list. All that the questions really ask is: "What is the job?" But they ask it in different ways. Some managers find that ideas are triggered when the question is asked in one way and some when it is given another way: What is the position's unique contribution? Why is the position needed at all? What would change if the position were eliminated? What will change if I am highly effective in the position? How would I know, with no one telling me, when I am performing effectively? What authority does the position really have? What do the job description and the organizational manual say? How do I spend my time? How should I like to spend my time? What would I be most likely to concentrate on over two or three years if I wanted to make the greatest improvement in my unit? in my superior's unit? in the organization as a whole?

GUIDES FOR TESTING EFFECTIVENESS AREAS

When effectiveness areas are identified, they should satisfy six tests which check on the adequacy of the effectiveness areas both individually and collectively. Each effectiveness area should: (1) represent output, not input; (2) lead to associated objectives which are measurable; (3) be an important part of the position; and (4) be within the actual limits of authority and responsibility.

Effectiveness areas as a whole should: (5) represent 100 percent of the outputs of the position, and (6) not be so numerous as to avoid dealing with the essence of the job or so few as to make planning difficult.

FLEXIBILITY OF EFFECTIVENESS AREAS

The manager at the top of any organizational unit usually has some flexibility in the choice of the effectiveness areas he decides to associate with his own position. This freedom is very marked when he has the ability to create a subordinate and can assign part of his own work to the subordinate. Under these conditions the top man's areas are fully flexible: he can make them what he wants to be. He could, for instance, become an "outside" man with an emphasis on liaison with other organizational units or customers. His newly created subordinate could be the "inside" man concerned with managing the unit. The reverse situation is equally feasible. This demonstrates clearly that, within broad limits, a manager who can create a subordinate and can design his subordinate's effectiveness areas has a very wide range of different areas which he can associate with his own job.

It is impossible to look at the effectiveness areas for a particular position in isolation. Such areas are best seen as sets of areas which link several positions together. It is quite possible, then, that if the set of areas for one position changes a great deal, sets of areas for other positions may change as well; and they should. When setting areas, then, the question is not "What are they?" but "What could they best be?" Clearly MBO is intimately related to organizational design and organizational flexibility.

A plant manager after three years on the job may well decide to change the effectiveness areas he established three years earlier. He may have trained one or more subordinates to assume some of them.

The important thing is that effectiveness areas should not simply be applied to an existing organizational design and then considered to be relatively permanent: instead, the assigning of effectiveness areas should be used as a basis for inducing organizational flexibility and seeing that it is maintained.

Effectiveness areas usually are subject to change when: a new manager is appointed, co-workers change, a manager grows in skill, power and decision levels move, MBO is implemented, or any major organizational change occurs.

MAKING MANAGERIAL EFFECTIVENESS OPERATIONAL

Managerial effectiveness should be linked directly to organization philosophy, induction training, and organization development. In this way it becomes the firm's central value induced by training and OD. Effectiveness areas should be the basis of describing job and of linking one job to another, that is, system design. Effectiveness standards form a basis for job specifications, what kind of manager is required; manager selection, is this the man we want; training plans, how do we obtain desired behavior; and job evaluation, how much should we pay. Objectives form the basis of the link between corporate strategy, and managerial appraisal. These four concepts then can provide the central theme for a philosophy of management.

PLANNING ANALYSIS—LOOKING AHEAD

Planning analysis is the first crucial step in the MBO/R Operation System. What is done at this stage is based on the foundation established in the navigation system of mission, roles, and effectiveness areas. This emphasizes the importance of planning in the MBO/R process. It is where the planning system in the organization is integrated with the MBO/R system. Many planning systems will include most of the same steps that we are advocating in an MBO/R system. It is not significant what terms or labels you put on these steps. The important thing is that they are followed.

The integration of planning and MBO/R is important to the success of each. An organization implementing MBO/R without planning will not bring about desired change, nor will planning alone accomplish it. Both of these concepts are based on three major assumptions: (1) change can be recognized, anticipated and influenced; (2) change can be managed; and (3) deliberate planning is basic to successful management.[1] We think that the planning analysis step forces management to manage the future by formulating objectives that are future-oriented rather than based chiefly on the past.

In this first step of the MBO/R operation system the following items should be included:

1) *Analyis of the Internal Environment* This will entail an analysis of the strengths and weaknesses of the organization and also the opportunities and threats facing it. The assessment of in-

ternal resources is reduced to manpower, financial, physical, and technical resources.[2]

2) *Appraisal of the External Environment* This includes those factors which affect the organization's, or unit's, success or failure. They will include general economic trends, government policies and regulations, the actions of competitors, technological advancements, and sociopolitical changes. The continuous and ongoing analysis of these external factors is essential to the survival and growth of organizations, whether they are profit-oriented or nonprofit-oriented.

3) *Analysis of the Organization's Past Performance* This should be done in each of the effectiveness areas[3] established.

4) *Assumptions about the Future* These assumptions will be about certain events in the future which may have an impact on the organization and its development of goals and objectives. They will include political, economic, scientific, cultural, social, and technological influences. The assumptions will, to a large extent, be judgmental and broad in nature, but to be meaningful they should have certain quantitative values or estimates of time and magnitude of occurrence.

With the data generated in these four areas and the MBO/R navigation system as a guide, management will be in a position to set long-range goals. These may be continuous in nature or limited in time to three, five, or ten years or whatever time period is a reasonable planning span for the organization. Examples of long-range goals would be: (1) "X" percent growth rate per year; or (2) R & D expenses held to a maximum percentage of sales. Examples of time-oriented, long-range goals would be: (1) a certain capability by "X" year; or (2) a certain size by "X" year. One sorting out process in developing these long-range goals is the asking of the following questions: (1) What can the organization do? (2) What might it do? (3) What does it want to do? and (4) What should or must it do?

Strategic planning is now possible to determine and evaluate alternative paths to the accomplishment of the mission and long-range goals. This offers the opportunity for maximum creativity and innovation—a highly synergistic process. The ability of management groups to achieve this is dependent on their ability to work together in an open, honest climate. There is an element of risk taking in strategic planning. The risks might be evaluated according to what the organization can afford to take, cannot afford to take because of its lack of resources or other reasons, and cannot afford not to take.[4]

Strategies need to be based on the strengths and resources of the organizations and should be in such areas as finance, marketing/product-reviews, manufacturing and operations, research and development, and general management.

There are many approaches to strategic planning depending on the organization. One unique approach that integrates it with MBO/R is practiced at Texas Instruments.[5]

PLANNING ANALYSIS AT ALL LEVELS

The planning analysis step needs to be accomplished at all levels in the organization but will take on a different form as it moves downward. Much of this chapter has been written from the standpoint of what needs to happen at the top management level. In our opinion this is where it starts and then should cascade down through the organization allowing for the same process to occur at each level. Traditionally, planning has taken place at the top management level or in a planning department, and then has been imposed in a directive way by managers spelling out how individuals were to carry out their function. There needs to be direction from above on What needs to be achieved, but there should be allowance for the Who and How to be worked at the lower levels. It is desirable to have a high level of participation in the planning analysis, but limited participation and high direction may be appropriate in some units depending on their most effective way of operating.

The planning analysis article by F.R. Hinton in this chapter will be helpful to managers at all levels in handling this step in the MBO/R process.

PLANNING ORGANIZATION

Planning is a specialty in itself and most organizations will find it necessary to have some technical planning help available for training, consultation, coordination, data gathering, and other support functions needed by the line organization to carry out the planning process. It is essential that planning personnel in the organization operate in a support capacity and do not usurp the responsibility of the line organization to develop the plans.

SUMMARY

As an organization moves more deeply into MBO/R, management will discover more need for an effective planning system and planning skills. If there is a planning system in operation, it will have to be integrated with the MBO/R system as soon as possible. The development of an effective planning system and its full integration with MBO/R may require several years.

Planning analysis is a vital link between mission, roles and effectiveness areas and the actual objective setting process. It is an ongoing function as a part of the recycling process of the MBO/R operation system and may occur out of sequence as needed. One of its chief contributions to the objective-setting process is that objectives will be set on the right things, the priority ones. These objectives will be future-oriented.

NOTES

1. G.M. Glavin 1974. "The management of planning: a third dimension of business planning." *The Business Quarterly* (Autumn), p. 44.
2. A.P. Raia 1974. *Managing by objectives.* Glenview, Ill.: Scott Foresman, p. 36.
3. Similar to and often considered the same as "key results areas" used in the following article by Frank R. Hinton.
4. L.J. Hughlett 1974. *Long-range planning implemented by management by objectives for results.* Boone, N. C.: Erdec Institute, p. 225.
5. G. Helms 1972. Texas instruments' OST system for managing innovation, *MBO Journal* (May), pp. 11-18.

PLANNING ANALYSIS

FRANK R. HINTON

The planning analysis, as the name suggests, is an assessment of performance and all related problems, changes, and conditions preparatory to making the planning decisions for the period ahead. To set realistic goals it is necessary to evaluate the present, study the past, and forecast the future. Accordingly, the analysis should include:

- An assessment of the gap between current and ideal performance.
- An analysis of changes necessary to improve performance.
- An analysis of all factors and changes likely to affect performance, including external changes, workload changes, and internal strengths and weaknesses.

With relation to the performance gap, "ideal" performance is that performance level which would be considered completely acceptable under normal conditions.

The assessment of this performance gap can obviously be only as good as the information available and this will depend upon the development of performance indicators and the feedback system. Most organizations, with or without planning systems, accumulate and report some performance data such as expenditures and staff levels. However, experience shows that until an emphasis on results brings the development of the Key Results Areas' measurement indicators, these data are often not relevant or adequate. Lacking suitable data and statistics on performance the manager can then make only a general assessment against each KRA based on observation and judgment supported by whatever factual evidence is available.

The assessment of the performance gap must also include an identification and analysis of the significant factors and problems

Reprinted with permission of Frank R. Hinton, Bureau of Management Consulting, Government of Canada.

affecting performance. This will mean establishing answers to such questions as the following:

"If no changes were made to my operations, what performance could I expect at the end of the period ahead?"

"What changes would I have to make to achieve a significant improvement to my performance?"

"What are the key problems currently affecting my performance?"

In assessing the need for improvements to performance and the factors and problems involved, it is also useful to look at the trends in performance and data on contributing factors. The study of trends involves the assembly of historical data and its analysis to determine if there are patterns emerging which have significance for the planning of future performance targets. Projection of these trends may also be most significant. For instance, equipment maintenance costs for a unit might show a steady increase in recent years which, if projected, would show a completely unacceptable level of costs a few years ahead. Analysis of the causes of the trend might identify problems important to the planning analysis such as operator misuse or equipment obsolescence.

Thus far the planning analysis has concentrated on the identification of performance deficiencies and the problems to do with improving performance. Logically it should next cover the analysis of the alternative means of improving performance. Logically it should next cover the analysis of the alternative means of improving performance with an estimate of the resources required by each. This should include the creative development of all practical solutions with all information necessary to the proper evaluation of each.

Next, in order to prepare for the comparative evaluation of the alternatives, an assessment must be made of all the factors which might influence the ability to improve performance. This should include forecasted changes to the work load, external changes or factors, and internal factors such as strengths or weaknesses and resourcing constraints. A simple way of recording these factors is by means of a "Force Field" chart as illustrated. This charting makes for easy visual review in considering their impact on the capability for performance improvement and on the choice between the alternative methods.

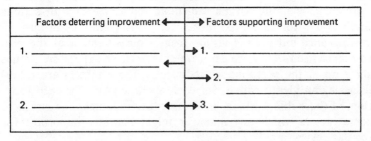

Force Field Analysis

The forecasting of future work load requires the estimating of the expected demands upon a component or organization for the services it provides or function it performs. In the short-range planning at lower levels this can be interpreted from the planning of the served components or from information obtained from them. In long-range planning this usually involves intensive studies of the department's or function's role and the future demands upon it.

Factors external to the component may also have a bearing on its performance and will therefore have to be considered in the planning analysis. Examples of these factors outside the department might be technical developments, economic, social and political developments, legislative changes, etc. Examples within the department but outside the component might be policy changes, role or organization changes to other sectors of the department, development of data processing systems, etc. Such factors may affect the future work-load requirements of the component, its facilities requirements, or present problems for the maintenance or improvement of performance. With short-range planning at lower levels identification and assessment of these factors can be made from knowledge of local conditions and information from associated components. With longer-range planning most organizations find it necessary to carry out extensive studies, particularly with respect to such "environmental" factors as social, technical, economic, and political developments and trends.

Internal strengths and weaknesses concern those internal conditions or factors which may affect a component's performance, particularly where the effect is delayed. For example, an age distribution study of the work force might show a large number of retirements pending without adequate replacements with serious implications for future performance. Such factors contribute to performance but are not visible from a measurement of the performance itself. They are causes, not effects, and therefore do not show up in the performance indicators. These factors are established by an identification, for each operation and for each function, of those things which could affect performance. For instance, some factors which any manager might consider important for regular review are:

- the development opportunities for employees
- internal versus external promotions
- generation of innovative or creative ideas
- obsolescence of equipment

The planning analysis, then, is seen to consider all those factors which could affect performance. Most managers would automatically consider many of these factors in their planning. However, it has been found by experience that the identification and formal consideration of them expands the analysis and raises additional significant considerations. The planning analysis is therefore an aid to the planner and identified as an integral element of the program.

OBJECTIVES: MANAGEMENT'S WORKING TOOL

The development of objectives, both organizational and personal, is the next step in the MBO/R operation system. Considering the MBO/R navigation system and the planning analysis, four steps have preceded the objective writing step. This is significant because we have found that the first step in many MBO installations is the writing of objectives. The danger of writing objectives immediately in the implementation process is that they may not be written on the right subjects, the priority items to produce organization RESULTS. They may also be based on past activities rather than on future achievement.

WHAT IS AN OBJECTIVE?

An objective is a statement of specific RESULTS (outputs) that an individual or a group plans to produce through their efforts (activities/inputs). It is a planned venture into time and space which draws on one's creative potential. A "good" objective should be RESULTS centered, measurable, time- and cost-bounded, realistic, desirable, and attainable.

While all of the steps in the MBO/R navigation/operation model may not be completed before objectives are written, management can be aware of these and proceed with what is feasible at a particular time. For instance, it may be a couple of years before management is able to go into depth in the planning analysis. The model can be helpful in planning the MBO/R implementation over several years.

The quantification of objectives may possibly be overemphasized to the extent that objectives that cannot be completely, or readily, quantified are not written. To help on this problem, the following phrase should be added to the word "measurable": "or at least observable and describable." If it is not possible at the time of writing an objective to develop a specific quantitative measure, it is possible to make a statement as to how the objective is going to be evaluated as to whether it is met or not. The standard of measurement may be a judgmental one and certain individuals will make this subjective evaluation. It must be determined at the time of writing the objective who will make the subjective evaluation and what criteria will be used. Quite often as the action plan is developed, progress will be made on meaningful standards for the hard-to-measure items. This difficulty is especially prevalent in the case of delivery of services. The response often heard is "We cannot evaluate our services." We suggest that this be turned around to "How are we going to evaluate our services?" When this approach is taken, the group generally will make progress in developing measurement criteria and standards.

A RESULTS-centered objective is written in terms of the end and not the means. To avoid the activity trap, we recommend that no action verbs be used in the objective. In the past it has been emphasized that objectives be written by starting with the word "to" and follow it with an action verb. For instance, the objective is "to reduce costs by 5 percent by December 31 with no additional expenditure of funds." We recommend dropping "to reduce," which denotes activity, and rewording the objective: "Costs at $X by December 31 with no additional expenditure of funds."

DETERMINATION OF OBJECTIVES TO BE DEVELOPED

Having identified both the effectiveness areas and effective measurement criteria and having worked through the planning analysis, individuals and groups are in a position to develop objectives. The steps prior to this one help groups and boss-subordinate pairs sort out the most important areas in which change is needed. Objectives will help bring about this needed change.

In the beginning we recommend only one objective per job and that it be a short-range one (60 to 90 days) and that there be a good chance to achieve it so that the manager of the objective experiences some success early. After working this way for several months, the number of objectives may be increased to two or more. Our recommendation is that one position not have more than five objectives at any one time.

One approach to developing objectives between boss and subordinate is the use of the model in Fig. 12.1.

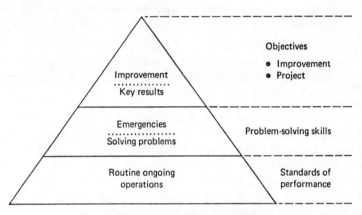

Fig. 12.1 Time analysis model. [1]

A manager's job can be broken down into (1) routine ongoing operations; (2) handling of emergencies and/or problem solving; and (3) improvement tasks. When the job is broken down into these three categories, the boss and subordinate are able to see where the subordinate's time is being spent and determine if this is the most effective use of time. At least 20 percent of a manager's time should be spent on improvement. If this is not the case, the boss and subordinate may set objectives to make changes in routine operating tasks and/or problem-solving tasks to make time available for improvement objectives. The proportion of time spent in these three categories will vary from one job to another and from one time period to another on the same job.

Standards of performance can be written for the routine operating parts of the job making it unnecessary to have objectives for these tasks. Some MBO texts label objectives in this area as routine, maintenance, or normal work output objectives.[2] (Standards of performance will be treated in Chapter 13). Consequently we see objectives being developed in the improvement area of the subordinate's job. These objectives could fall into two broad categories:

1) *Improvement objectives*—will be concerned with a part of the job that, when achieved, will increase the effectiveness of the subordinate.

2) *Project objectives*—may be on a special task that the subordinate has total responsibility for or as a part of a project team involving personnel from different units. These may be in the area of innovation or problem solving.

One distinct advantage in using the model in Fig. 12.1 is that it maintains a balanced approach to an individual's job. It is possible to become so gung ho on objectives with the emphasis on "winning" that routine operating and problem-solving parts of the job are ignored or slighted. Part of this total managing process is the ability to maintain a level of acceptable performance on routine matters, take care of problem-solving emergencies effectively, and devote 20 percent or more time to innovative improvement work.

PERSONAL OBJECTIVES

The objectives described thus far have been organizational, or work, objectives. A basic part of the MBO/R concept is the development of personal objectives for each person. This is critical for integrating the needs of individuals with the needs of the organization so that there is a high degree of satisfaction on both sides.

It is essential that the boss be aware of the personal and career goals of the subordinate so that he can be as supportive as possible in helping the subordinate achieve them while he is accomplishing organization objectives. These may be modified in the negotiation between boss and subordinate in the goal setting process. We think it is just as important to develop personal objectives for the development of the employee as it is to set organizational objectives. These may be written in areas such as skill development, technical knowledge, and development of competencies supportive of career goals. Others may be written in areas of personal growth and related subjects supportive of the individual's life plan. Once these are set and there is agreement between the boss and subordinate, there should be the same accountability for achievement as on organizational objectives.

OBJECTIVE SETTING PROCESS

The interface between boss and subordinate, between team and individuals, and between boss and team is the core of the objective setting process. This is an "eyeball-to-eyeball" negotiation process in a climate of openness. This is necessary for the needs of the organization and individuals to be fully considered and for commitment to the objectives developed.[3]

Realistically this process probably will never work 100 percent. There will be times when the individual will not agree with the organizational objectives, but will accept and support them because there is freedom in how they are achieved and/or freedom to achieve personal objectives in other areas. There will also be some organizational objectives that will not be negotiable. However, there usually is freedom for negotiation on how they will be accomplished. Also there will be times when it may be difficult, or impossible, for an individual to achieve his personal objectives in the organization. This needs to be openly addressed so that the individual can make the decision to change his objectives, accept the fact that he cannot meet them, or make a change in jobs in the organization or elsewhere so he can achieve his career and life aspirations.

The importance of the face-to-face negotiation of objectives cannot be overemphasized. Unfortunately in some MBO systems only the organizational objectives from above are considered and these are passed down to the individual or team with no input from them. Another approach, equally inappropriate, is when the boss asks his subordinates for their objectives without giving them his and/or the organization's objectives. The first is a top-down only approach and the second is a bottom-up only. We think each way is dysfunctional because the expectations from above or below are not considered, and there is not the interface at each level. From an organizational standpoint, it is best that it start at the top with top management making visible its expectations and the two-way (down and up) process work from there. In working this vertical process, it is mandatory that the objectives also be worked horizontally at all levels in order that conflicts in objectives can be resolved.

Many MBO systems are limited to boss-subordinate objective setting. An individual's effectiveness in the organization can be diminished or lost if the horizontal interface does not take place. This horizontal action needs to take place among the team members and may also be appropriate with other units in the organization. This eliminates conflicting objectives and ensures integration of individual objectives into organizational objectives.

This face-to-face negotiation process between boss and subordinate and the team is likely to present problems. There is considerable risk involved, and it may be threatening to some individuals. If this is the situation, consulting help should be available to assist individuals and groups in developing the interpersonal skills to work together effectively, handle conflicts positively, and manage accountability.

NOTES

1. M. Kellogg. Performance Appraisal Seminar, University of Richmond. A similar model is presented by George Odiorne 1965, in *Management by objectives,* Pitman, pp. 98–126.
2. G.L. Morrisey 1970., *Management by objectives and results.* Reading, Mass.: Addison-Wesley, pp. 42–43.
3. A.C. Beck, Jr., and E.D. Hillmar 1972. *A practical approach to organization development through MBO,* Reading, Mass.: Addison-Wesley, p. 230.

WRITING MEASURABLE OBJECTIVES FOR STAFF MANAGERS

BY DALE D. McCONKEY

Pity the poor staff manager! So goes the thinking in many organizations. He deals in intangibles and he's there to provide service and advice to his line associates. Neither his mission nor his contributions can be measured. He's a complete nonentity in many instances—tolerated because of the occasional need for his specialized knowledge or an administrator of routine, ongoing activities—but often receiving neither the opportunity to make a profit-oriented contribution nor acceptance and recognition for his accomplishments when they are achieved.

Fortunately the "poor" staff manager need be pitied no longer. The advanced applications of Management by Objectives (or Management by Results as it is often termed) now permit the staff manager to write measurable objectives to measure rather finitely his contributions compared to his objectives, to receive deserved recognition in the process, and to take his proper place as a member of the profit-making team. Concurrently, the staff manager's organization receives value due for its money and begins to eliminate the management void which has existed since World War I.

This has been a most costly void and resulted from the failure to measure staff managers and hold them accountable for achieving specific, profit-oriented results. The key to solving the problem lies in writing measurable objectives for those managers working in the so-called staff departments or functions of: personnel and labor relations, public relations, finance, law, research and development, engineering, purchasing, marketing services, industrial engineering, and others.

WRITING MEASURABLE OBJECTIVES:

The paramount difficulty in writing staff objectives is overcoming the long-practiced misconception that they cannot be measured—

not in writing measurable objectives. Under MBO they can and must be measurable. To admit otherwise would be tantamount to agreeing that 20 to 40 percent of the average company's manpower budget is being expended on staff functions which can't be measured and that companies, therefore, must rely upon some form of divine guidance to make certain they are receiving value due for these tremendous expenditures. It should suffice to say that a company would be extremely reluctant to approve such amounts for any other type of project without first determining the rather finite measurements by which its return on investment would be gauged.

Take for example an organization whose "general and administrative expense" budget, exclusive of items such as interest on debt and other nonmanpower items, approximates $2 million—a not uncommon situation. Further, assume the percentage of staff costs of this figure is only 20 percent. Thus, we are talking about a cost of $400,000 for the costs of staff managers and the matters for which they recommend, secure approval, and ultimately control. Now, this expenditure of $400,000 will be relabeled to change its cost classification and to illustrate the measures which would be required if it were, for example, a request for new equipment.

Before the company approves the expenditure it would want to know, at the very minimum: the details of how, when, and for what the money would be used; the advantages of the new equipment over the old; the financial worth of these advantages; and the return on investment for the $400,000.

Assume a production manager walks into his boss's office and asks for $400,000 to buy new equipment; he tells his boss that it is impossible to determine or measure what return the organization will receive on its two-fifths of a million dollars of investment. The reader can image what would happen in his particular organization. In the first instance, no production manager worth his salt would ever make such a request. In the second instance, and in the unlikely event he did, his request would be turned down out-of-hand and his name would be moved to the bottom of the promotion list. If the company continued to retain him in employment, he would probably spend his next few weeks attending classes on basic business techniques for the student manager. Yet, a company is guilty of exactly this when it approves the same expense for staff managers who have objectives or responsibilities which are considered incapable of being measured.

The indictment that staff objectives could not be measured was valid prior to MBO because prior to MBO these objectives, at best, were "for motherhood and against sin" types of objectives. They often read as follows:

1. To attain and maintain the highest possible degree of quality (for a quality control manager).

2. To provide expert financial and accounting advice (for a financial manager).

3. To design a product of the greatest consumer appeal at the lowest cost of production (for a design engineer).

4. To formulate and recommend programs which will promote employee interest and morale (for a personnel manager).

5. To purchase raw materials and supplies in accordance with specifications (for a purchasing manager).

6. To advise and counsel the company's managers in the preparation of both short- and long-range plans as an aid in achieving the company's objectives (for a planning manager).

7. To support the production department by providing well thought out recommendations on matters such as operational layout, work flow, and manufacturing processes (for an industrial engineering manager).

8. To enhance the company's image in the eyes of the buying public by securing the placement of publicity favorable to the company in media such as newspapers, magazines, radio and television (for a public relations manager).

DETERMINING STAFF'S MISSION

The staff manager must give considerable thought to his true mission in the organization before he can write worthwhile objectives. The failure of the staff manager to make this determination usually will result in his compiling a list of routine activities which he plans to pursue. For example, the true mission of an advertising manager is not to formulate and administer advertising programs;

his real job is to help generate sales by the type, manner, and cost of the advertising effort he completes. In similar fashion, the mission of the research manager is not to spend money carrying out research activities but to add to sales and profits by developing new products or improving old ones. An industrial engineer's job is not to conduct efficiency studies but to help increase production output. The major difference in all three of these examples is the distinct demarcation which must be established between merely pursuing activities and achieving specific results. Two examples will illustrate the importance of this difference for a staff engineering manager.

In the first example, the engineering manager considers his mission as being "to provide engineering services to the operating divisions." When he writes his so-called objectives he will undoubtedly end up with a lengthy list of activities designed to carry out his mission: it would be all but impossible to arrive at any other type of objectives because he has cast his mission as an activity. In the second example, the engineering manager states his mission in terms of the results he must achieve to justify his existence. His mission states that he is accountable for "effecting savings in plant and equipment costs through achieving X, Y, and Z results." An actual engineering objective covered by the second example reads as follows:

> Reduce design engineering and manufacturing cost ratio to total equipment and rebuild cost from present 17.3% to 15% without reducing quality of design and manufacture of equipment.

Thus, before staff managers can consider writing meaningful, measurable objectives, they must arrive at an understanding of their true mission. The failure to do so will result in objectives that are not specific and not responsive to the real needs of the organization.

QUALITATIVE TO QUANTITATIVE OBJECTIVES

Prior to the extensive use of MBO it was usually believed, and practiced, that line managers should have quantitative objectives, i.e., those dealing with numbers such as sales figures, cost levels, ratios, return on investment, quotas, and profits. It was assumed, and widely practiced, that staff managers who dealt in intangibles could not have quantitative objectives but only qualitative ones in which the manager tried to state as specifically as possible that which he was going to accomplish. Even though it is still necessary for the staff manager to rely sometimes on specific, qualitative objectives, staff objectives are moving more and more to the quantified type. Following are two examples which illustrate the movement from qualitative to quantitative type objectives. The first one is a general corporate objective; the second is a specific staff objective:

Example 1, A General Corporate Objective: Companies have long appreciated the value of having a quality reputation for their products. It builds customer confidence, sales, and profits. Thus, companies frequently established an objective dealing with product quality. It usually reads along the following lines:

> Our objective is to achieve the number one quality reputation for our company within the industry.

At best, this was a qualitative type of objective and, while highly laudable, it could not be measured. No definition of quality had been agreed to and it was not possible to determine when or if the objective ever was reached. It was a "for motherhood" type of objective. Before it could become a meaningful objective in accordance with MBO it was necessary to define what the objective meant and how it was to be measured. The period of roughly the last eight years has seen organizations make dramatic strides in solving both the definition and measurement problems. This was accomplished by including in the objective *those specific conditions or indicators which must be met when in the judgment of management the objective had been satisfactorily accomplished.* Using this technique, the preceding quality reputation objective is now restructured as follows:

> Our objective is to achieve the number one quality reputation for our company in the industry. This objective will be accomplished when:

1. The number of field service calls does not exceed X percent.
2. The in-plant reject rate is X percent or less.

3. Warranty costs are less than X percent of sales.

4. Labor and materials cost for rework does not exceed X percent.

5. The company's product is rated in the first two positions for at least eight out of ten times in the monthly issues of *Consumer Highlights* magazine.

This objective, which always was one of the most nebulous ones, now is a very specific one which can be measured quite readily. Managers know what must be done to accomplish the objective and at the end of the target period they will know whether or not they have accomplished it.

Example 2, For a Staff Manager: Now the same procedure, as illustrated in the preceding example, will be applied to a personnel manager's accountability for training and development. His mission is not to "conduct training and development programs," but to actually train a certain number of employees according to standards which will achieve certain specified results.

Prior to MBO, this manager's qualitative objective probably read:

To formulate and conduct training programs to ensure the availability of trained personnel to meet the company's manpower requirements.

As was the case in the preceding example, this objective suffers from the lack of definition as to what was meant and some method of measuring whether or not it is accomplished. It moves from qualitative to quantitative status when it is restructured as follows:

To meet manpower requirements of the company by formulating and conducting training programs which will achieve the following results:

1. A replacement has been trained and is qualified for promotion for each job at Salary Level 15 or above.

2. Three graduate mechanical engineers are capable of promotion to the Senior Level.

3. Twelve foremen have completed and achieved a grade of 80 or better in the course, Basic Supervisory Techniques for Foremen.

4. At least 4 stationary engineers have completed the necessary training and have secured the license for First Class.

5. Twenty clerk-typist trainees have completed typing Course A and are able to type copy at the rate of at least 50 words per minute.

Here again, this objective illustrates how a general, qualitative one can be highly quantified and made into a meaningful, measurable objective. This procedure will be illustrated further with a few brief examples for other staff managers.

Credit Manager.   This manager's true mission is to generate increased sales through the manner in which he extends credit and collects accounts receivable. Both of these functions can exert a significant impact on profits. If he is too strict when approving credit, he can cost the company increased sales. On the other hand, a larger amount of bad debts may result if credit is extended too loosely. He can cost the company money which it could earn from interest if collections are not made on time. Thus, the conditions which he must meet, to adequately perform his job, might be spelled out as follows:
The credit manager will have performed his job in a satisfactory manner when:

1. Credit limits have been established for all accounts.

2. Credit applications are approved or disapproved within two days of receipt in 98 percent of the cases.

3. Accounts receivable are collected within 30 days for 60 percent of outstanding receivables and 45 days for 38 percent of receivables.

4. Bad debts do not exceed two percent of sales for the year.

5. No loss of sales result from the above.

Development Engineering Manager.   The qualitative objective for this manager usually would dwell upon his responsibility for designing and developing products and processes. His true mission is to enhance profits by the manner in which he runs his function and his profit contributing role is clear when spelled out as follows:

The manager of development engineering will have performed satisfactorily when he achieves the following results:*

1. Development costs are within a plus or minus 5 percent of budget for 98 percent of projects.

2. At least three new products reach the commercial stage and each achieves the sales and returns specified by company policy.

3. Savings of at least $50,000 are realized through the improvement of present products. These savings may result from reductions in labor, materials, or equipment.

4. Move Project A to a position where a "go" or "no go" decision may be made by September 1.

In summary, often a staff objective can be changed from a qualitative type to a quantitative one by first deciding the specific result which is desired and then listing or describing the specific conditions which will have been met when management considers the requirements of the objective to be satisfied.

MAKING OBJECTIVES SPECIFIC

Although it is desirable to quantify staff objectives as much as it is prudent to do so, it is not always possible or prudent to insist upon complete quantification.

In terms of being prudent, it is more worthwhile to the company to approve an objective of considerable importance even though the objective can be quantified to a lesser degree than it is to approve an objective of lesser worth which can be quantified to a greater degree. Assume for example, a financial manager having responsibility for financial forecasting and forms control. It is more difficult to quantify an objective covering financial forecasting than

---

*Many development projects require more than one year to reach fruition and usually the objective covers more than the one-year period used in this illustration.

one covering forms control. If the company insists upon extensive quantification, the financial manager might be prone to recommend an objective, and a highly quantified one, which provides he will reduce the cost of printing forms by 5 percent. He doesn't recommend one for financial forecasting because it would be more difficult to structure.

The insistence on extensive quantification, in this example, has cost the company money as the savings from not printing forms may have equaled a few hundred dollars while the loss through not pushing improved financial forecasting may have cost thousands of dollars or more. The same reasoning is applicable in the instance of a personnel manager who recommends an objective to reduce by X mills the unit cost of paper cups used in the cafeteria but doesn't recommend an objective covering a much needed compensation plan because the latter is more difficult to quantify.

Nor is it always possible to completely quantify staff objectives. To insist upon complete quantification in those instances in which it is not possible will not result in better objectives but it will result in much wasted effort by staff managers as they try to do the impossible and their faith and value in the MBO system will suffer. Like many facets of the management process, there are no clean-cut and ironclad rules as to the dividing line separating overquantification from lack of quantification. This is a matter which each organization and its managers must decide. However, there are a few proven ground rules which will, when followed, help to make any objective more specific in terms of definition and measurability.

Results, not Activities. Staff managers can improve their objectives appreciably by wording the objective in terms of the result they plan to achieve rather than the activities in which they will engage. It is far better to describe results, even though the result itself may not be capable of one hundred percent accuracy in definition, than to talk about activities. Examples of both are:

Activity— To conduct market research studies to improve the sale of company products.

Result— To select by July 1 three test markets for testing new Product B.

Who, What, and When.   Another technique for making objectives more specific is to make certain they include a clear statement of what is going to be accomplished, who is going to accomplish it, and when it is going to be accomplished. These are the three salient points of any delegation and should certainly be included in the objectives of an MBO system which essentially is a system for delegating the responsibility for results through all levels of management.

Avoid Relative Terms.   There is a tendency, especially concerning staff objectives which cannot always be quantified completely, to lapse into the expediency of using relative terms to describe results. Words such as adequate, sufficient, and reasonable are poor substitutes for more descriptive ones; they lead to countless misunderstandings and make measuring practically impossible. Consider the word "sufficient." What does it mean? Does it mean the same to all people? Can the magnitude of results be measured? Is it a sufficient standard against which to reward or discipline a manager? Can it be used to prepare a financial plan?

All relative terms should be replaced with more precise ones even though the more precise words still may fall short of complete precision. For example, instead of using the relative word "reasonable," state the result within parameters: even wide parameters are preferable to the relative word. Examples:

Poor — To achieve a reasonable improvement in the time required to prepare and distribute the Monthly Report of Operations.

Better— To reduce by 5 to 15 percent the time required to prepare and distribute the monthly report of operations.

Poor — To effect as much reduction as possible in the cost of operating the Law Department.

Better— To reduce the cost of operating the Law Department by 10 to 30 percent.

Poor — To direct the quality assurance function in a manner *sufficient* to meet anticipated needs.

Better— To improve product quality by recommending inspection procedures designed to detect 80 percent of substandard products.

The reader will note that none of the alternatives termed "better" are perfect; however, they are infinitely more valid as objectives than the ones which included relative terminology.

Management by Objectives provides the staff manager with the vehicle and opportunity of gaining acceptance of his function and recognition of his contributions. MBO provides the opportunity only. The degree to which the manager capitalizes on this opportunity depends in large part on how adept he becomes in structuring measurable objectives. To accomplish this he must first determine what his true mission is within the organization (for what is he really accountable) and then translate this accountability into specific, realistic, and measurable objectives which play their proper role in achieving the objectives of all other departments and the overall objectives of the organization.

STANDARDS OF PERFORMANCE—
THE BASIS FOR EVALUATION

While standards of performance is the next step in the MBO/R operation system, they may be developed before or during the objective setting step. Each objective should have a standard of performance.

A performance standard is defined as description of output conditions that will exist when a job is being performed *acceptably*. It represents the dividing line between success and failure, and provides the means for making self-control an actuality. Standards are performance factors expressed in terms of quantity, quality, time, and/or cost. They may be either positive or negative. Some typical units used are dollars and cents, numbers, percentages, ratios, degrees, and days/hours/minutes/seconds.[1]

Occasionally standards have to be stated in subjective terms. These may be called judgmental standards. They usually require more effort to develop and, for this reason, are not used very often. This is especially true in the area of service delivery and managing. The defense is "We cannot measure what we do." We suggest turning this statement around to "How are we going to measure the services delivered?" or "How are we going to evaluate the way we manage?" Measurement is essential if what we do is important. If it is not measured, the question must be asked, "Should we be doing it?"

Goal Analysis by R.F. Mager is recommended as a good reference to help in the development of standards in hard-to-measure areas. His "Hey Dad Test" and goal analysis procedure are especially helpful in developing observable RESULTS-oriented behavior in goal statements.[2]

SETTING STANDARDS

Standards of performance should be set in each effectiveness area. This ensures that there will be standards in all areas that RESULTS are necessary for organizational effectiveness.

It is possible to overdo standards of performance. As one plant manager remarked, "Don't mention standards to me. We have 200 of them. They're running out of our ears." The name of the game in that manager's organization was to find out which standards management was going to enforce at a given point in time.

The process for setting standards is the same used for setting objectives. Management needs to give employees their expectations and needs, and employees need to tell management what they can do with the available resources. This provides the data necessary for the negotiation process. It must be recognized that there will be minimum standards that are not negotiable. As stated earlier, the "how" of meeting them and the resources available usually are negotiable. The negotiation process, as stated in Chapter 12, is neither top-down nor bottom-up—it is both ways. In addition to the negotiation of standards between boss and subordinate, it is also essential that they be negotiated horizontally between peers to ensure compatibility and support.

MANAGING STANDARDS AND OBJECTIVES

In Chapter 12 we advocated limiting the number of objectives on any one job at any one time to two to five. This is possible by using standards of performance as a means of maintaining acceptable performance on routine operations. Objectives will be written only when a standard is being developed or changed, or when there is a special task to be achieved.

Standards of performance provide the means for making self-control an actuality. The plan-do-control model developed by Scott Myers shows how a group or an employee manages a job.[3] They know on what basis their performance is evaluated and the limits under which they are operating. They are responsible for planning, problem solving, decision making, and utilization of resources; they are then responsible for carrying out their plans and decisions; and in the third step receive feedback so that they can evaluate their performance against the agreed upon standards. They are accountable for making corrections when performance is below standard. This plan-do-control managing process is automatically carried out repeatedly by repairmen (auto mechanics, plumbers, and electricians), farmers, and individuals manufacturing a complete product. Achieving this process on most jobs can be accomplished with negotiated standards of performance and appropriate feedback systems that enable the individual or group to evaluate their performance. This is a way of determining the freedom that one has to perform a job. When negotiated it clarifies responsibility and is a basis for managing accountability. Feedback systems will be discussed in more detail in Chapter 15.

NOTES

1. A.C. Beck, Jr., and E.D. Hillmar 1972. *A practical approach to organization development through MBO—Selected readings.* Reading, Mass.: Addison-Wesley, pp. 248-255.

2. R.F. Mager 1972. *Goal analysis.* Belmont, Calif.: Fearon.

3. Beck, *op. cit.,* pp. 31-33.

NOW HERE'S MY PLAN—
PLANNING AND MANAGING THE ACTION

It has been said that an objective without an action plan is no more than a dream, or a forecast. The action plan is a detailed plan and schedule, developed in advance, of how the individual or group is going to accomplish an objective. It may be called a work plan or operation plan.

A detailed action plan will validate an objective as to whether it is feasible and achievable. As those responsible for carrying it out develop the action plan, the resources (personnel, material, and economic) needed and the barriers to achievement will be identified. Also, this process involving those persons needed to achieve the objective will result in a higher commitment on their part and consequently in a higher chance of success. This data will enable the manager of the objective to compete more favorably for limited resources.

DEVELOPMENT OF ACTION PLANS

After an objective is written, the person responsible for the objective starts the detailed planning process. If it is an objective that he will accomplish without help from others, he will develop the action plan and submit it to his boss and it will be between him and the boss from that point forward. If it is an organizational objective calling for the efforts of a number of people and/or units, the person responsible for the objective (objective manager) will start the strategic planning with a representative group of those who are needed to accomplish the result desired. It has been our experience that there are few objectives that can be accomplished by one individual without help from others except where the objective is a detailed part of an action plan on a larger objective.

The strategic planning process is similar to that described in Chapter 11 on planning analysis. In establishing strategies for each objective the objective manager and his group develop a master plan of resource needs, availability, and utilization to accomplish the objectives. Obstacles and outside influences are identified and alternative approaches are developed. The individuals and units needed will be drawn into the action planning process in the early stages to gain their input and their commitment to the objective. On a large objective there will be a hierarchy in the action plan with the group under the objective manager having subobjectives. Each person responsible for a subobjective may have individuals under him with tasks (subobjectives to them at this level). This breakdown should continue until the level of subobjectives comes out to be a task for an individual.

The interaction in this action planning stage can be highly synergistic leading to results above expectations. This is necessary because to meet a challenging objective, group members are going to have to do some new and different things. They must be creative and innovative because when they start they may not know how they are going to meet the objective. If the objective can be achieved without their doing anything different, there is no challenge. On the other hand, if the objective is set so high that there is little chance (for instance, a 10 percent chance), there is little challenge as no one expects achievement.

CHECKPOINTS

As the action plan is developed it will include checkpoints which are specific dates that a subobjective, or a designated part, will be completed. It is a time that the person responsible for a subobjective will report the status of his task to others. These checkpoints should be frequent, i.e., two to four weeks apart.

The final action plan will be a schedule of dates with some elements of the plan being carried out concurrently and others sequentially. It may be helpful to chart the steps using systems such as Critical Path, PERT and Gantt.

Checkpoint performance, if frequently reviewed in group meetings, will include many of the elements of progress review as discussed in Chapter 15. The amount of time devoted to checkpoint meetings will vary according to what has to be reported and discussed. Meetings may take 15 minutes or they may take several hours, depending on problems to be solved or changes to be made.

When individuals are committed to meet checkpoint dates, they are expected to meet them. However, if unforeseen delays or obstacles occur, the pending delay should be reported immediately by the individual responsible in order that his boss and/or team members have an opportunity to problem solve the delay. This may result in committing more resources, or adjusting the schedule. The worst thing that a manager of a subobjective can do is to surprise others at a checkpoint meeting with a delay or obstacle he has been aware of for weeks. The boss and peers do not appreciate "surprises."

This is one place where accountability must be managed. When an individual does not meet his commitments, he is confronted by his boss and/or peers. The approach needs to include "How can this nonperformance or substandard performance be prevented in the future?" but the current situation must be worked including any appropriate disciplinary action.

In managing an objective in this manner, a manager is performing his traditional management functions of planning, organizing, motivating, and controlling.

COMMITMENT OF RESOURCES

The action plan will denote in detail the resources that will have to be committed. This necessarily will have to be linked with strategic planning. The integration of detail budgeting into MBO/R takes place at this stage. This is discussed in some detail in "The Position and Function of Budgets in an MBO System" by Dale D. McConkey later in this chapter.

The individuals' commitments will be spelled out by the steps, or subobjectives, for which they are responsible. This then becomes a part of the individuals' job performances for which they are accountable to their boss as well as to the manager of the objective. In many cases the manager of the objective and the boss will be the same person.

RECYCLING OF OBJECTIVES

In the action planning process it may become evident that the objective is not a feasible one or that there needs to be other things accomplished prior to carrying out the action plan. In this case it will be appropriate to recycle to the planning analysis or objective setting stage for additional work and possibly the setting of other objectives. In the event that it is decided not to proceed with an objective because of insufficient resources, it may be appropriate to put it on the shelf and go into planning analysis. Other alternatives may be a scaling down of the magnitude of the objective or an extension of the time frame.

The development of action plans for an objective is one of the time shocks in the MBO/R process. It is time consuming and does require an additional time commitment in the early stages. For this reason it is advisable to work on only one objective at a time in the early months of implementation. The process will also move more slowly until managers learn the skills of managing this way. The payoffs for this time commitment are increased RESULTS in the long run, higher commitment on the part of all concerned, a saving of time in the long run, and effective use of resources.

PITFALLS IN ACTION PLANNING

In summary, some of the pitfalls, or errors, in action planning are: (1) devoting insufficient time to it; (2) not involving those needed to carry out the plan; (3) steps not broken down in sufficient detail, or not specific enough; (4) disregard for checkpoints, or not holding people accountable for meeting dates; (5) allowing the plan to become an end in itself and not focusing on getting the job done; (6) not recognizing that some activities can go on concurrently; (7) failure to review progress at intervals; (8) failure to evaluate performance whether objective is met or not met; and (9) failure to be aware of the group process in goal setting and checkpoint meetings.[1]

This is another important point in the MBO/R process where it is essential that there be an open climate so that emPOWERment can take place.

NOTE

1. W.J. Reddin 1971. *Effective management by objectives*. New York: McGraw-Hill, p. 96.

THE POSITION AND FUNCTION OF BUDGETS IN AN MBO SYSTEM

DALE D. McCONKEY

Of all the questions raised by the dramatic growth of Management by Objectives few are more indicative of disorganized confusion than those relating to the position and role of budgets in an MBO system. The following are but a few of the situations faced by the author in recent months:

Company A The president indicated that the company had been operating with MBO for two years and now believed it was time to implement a budget system.

> *Comment:* Budgets are an integral part of an MBO system and the company could not have been practicing MBO without them.

Company B This company followed the practice of approving budgets during February of each year and then having its managers write their objectives during the ensuing six months.

> *Comment:* The budget is on the wrong end of the planning objective setting process. Budgets should conclude, not begin, the

process. There is little basis on which to approve the budgets unless the objectives and plans have been formulated.

Organization C Every two years the head of a Canadian government department is required to submit and defend the budget for his operations at a "budget justification" meeting. He inquired as to whether or not it would be a good idea to also have his objectives and plans prepared and available for the same meeting.

Comment: Objectives and plans are the only way the budget can be "justified." Without the objectives and plans, the budget cannot be tested for realism.

Company D The senior management team was thoroughly convinced it was operating under an MBO system simply because all operations were covered by operating expense and capital budgets.

Comment: Budgets are only one part of an MBO system. By themselves they're usually a sterile exercise in compiling numbers—an exercise in futility.

Organization E The head of this social agency had issued instructions to his managers that the budget should cover only the objectives of each manager. If a subject was not covered by an objective, it should not be included in the budget.

Comment: Budgets cover more than just objectives because the latter are usually limited to priority matters. Routine matters are not covered by objectives but the cost of the routine is reflected in the budget.

Organization F In the early days of an MBO installation, it was found that this organization had three different budgets intended to serve three different purposes—financial planning, motivation, and control.

Comment: One budget, properly designed and constructed, should serve all three purposes.

All of the above reveal a rather alarming amount of misconception and confusion regarding the role of budgets. Also, they indicate the failure of many organizations to update the traditional approach to budgeting to make it compatible with an MBO system. The resulting void has a major impact on the effectiveness of the MBO efforts.

Budgets have a key role to play, but only when this role is thoroughly understood and budgets are placed in their proper position. Otherwise, they operate to the detriment of MBO.

TRADITIONAL BUDGETING IS OBSOLETE

The impact of twenty years of widespread practice of Management by Objectives has brought about dramatic changes in the traditional practice of management. Many parts of the management process have been rendered obsolete.* The latter includes the traditional view of budgeting and its relationship to planning.

Commonly, budgets have been looked upon as "a plan or estimate of future income and expenses." They were heavily oriented to control.

An excellent example of the traditional approach to planning and budgeting is illustrated by the following case involving a university chancellor:

The date is July 20, 1973, and one of the chancellors of a large university is conducting his annual planning session for the 1974 year.

He announces that the total budget for 1974 for all units under his direction will be $10 million allocated individually as follows:

Director of Housing	$ 2 million
Director of Program Development	1 million
Director of Communications Center	3 million
Director of Residence Halls	1 million
Director of Testing Program	2 million
Chancellor's Office	1 million
TOTAL	**$10 million**

The 1974 budgetary figure represents a reduction of 10 percent from 1973 levels in accordance with a mandate from Governor I.B.

---

*For an in-depth treatment of this impact, see Dale D. McConkey, MBO - Twenty years later, where do we stand? *Business Horizons* **14**, (August), 1973.

Good to increase the productivity of all state activities by a comparable amount.

The chancellor provides the following ground rules to his department heads for their guidance when preparing their plans for 1974:

a. Emphasis will be on increased productivity.

b. There will be no lessening of quality standards.

c. Budgetary allocations will be adhered to strictly, both in total and by individual units.

d. Final budgets are due on September 1, 1973.

The chancellor concludes the meeting with a pep talk about the satisfaction derived from doing a job well under trying circumstances.

Each of the Directors submitted his budget and the final budget was assembled on September 1. It reflected the following:

Recommended Budget

Director of Housing	$ 2 million
Director of Program Development	1 million
Director of Communications Center	3 million
Director of Residence Halls	1 million
Director of Testing Program	2 million
Chancellor's Office	1 million
TOTAL	**$10 million**

The chancellor commended his staff for their planning expertise.

As do most traditionalists, this chancellor has made several telling mistakes—all of which will decrease his effectiveness as well as that of his organization. First, his approach precluded any but a cursory participation on the part of his managers. They parroted back to him what they assumed were predetermined figures and what their boss wanted to hear. Second, he deliberately refused to establish any competition among his managers for the available capital. Those who had been guilty of operating inefficiently in the past were given the same consideration as those who had been breaking their backs and operating in a highly effective manner.

Thus, emphasis was placed on spending the money made available—not on optimizing results. Third, the chancellor has positioned the budget on the wrong end of his so-called planning process. He's assigned a cost allowance to each manager without first giving any consideration to priorities and what *should* be done during the year. Fourth, in the chancellor's approach, controlling took priority over motivating managers to greater accomplishment.

UPDATING BUDGET'S PURPOSE

The purpose and role of budgets must undergo considerable updating if budgets are to perform their required role—and it is a most important one—within an MBO system.

Budgets must be primarily viewed as "the planned allocation of resources to the manager's objectives." This is more than a change in definition! It involves an entirely new way of looking at budgets and their role.

Also, it requires viewing the very role of management in a new light. The true role of a manager can be viewed as "optimizing the return on the resources entrusted to him." It is the total optimization of all of a company's resources (capital, people, plant and equipment) by all of its managers which, in the last analysis, determines the success of the organization. Resources available to an individual manager are always limited in a healthy organization. A company which doesn't establish competition for its resources is a sick company as is a company which has more resources than it knows what to do with. Therefore, an effective planning and budgeting approach should always promote competition among its managers for the available resources. Except in those rare instances where exigencies of the moment may dictate a different priority, the available (and always limited) resources should be awarded to the manager who can justify a return of twelve percent on the resources in contrast to another manager whose objective will return only eight percent.

The revised definition and approach to budgeting means that:

a. The formulation of objectives and plans precedes the preparation of the budget.

b. Objectives are based on a priority of needs of the organization.

c. Each manager is given the opportunity to compete for available resources by demonstrating what he will do with the resources if they are awarded to him.

Thus, from an MBO viewpoint, budgets in their simplest form are the quantification in dollars and cents of what the objectives and plans of all managers viewed collectively mean in profit and/or loss for the target period.

Now let's return to the university chancellor and examine the manner in which he could have used the MBO approach to optimize his results.

His first remedial step would be to begin his process earlier in the year, say in January or February of 1973 when preparing plans for 1974. This earlier start will permit additional dialogue between him and his directors and among the directors themselves on major points which they must coordinate with each other.

Next he would not begin his briefing by assigning each of the directors a budget allocation. Instead, he would provide his directors with the ground rules within which they would do their planning. These ground rules might include the following:

a. Emphasis will be on increased return on the resources used.

b. Each director will submit specific objectives covering the major results he plans to achieve.

c. All objectives must be supported by concrete plans for achievement.

d. All plans and objectives must be justified to the maximum extent possible.

e. One overall organizational objective is to lower total expenditures by the maximum extent possible consistent with contribution.

f. First draft of objectives and plans is due by March 15, 1973.

g. Final allocation of resources will be based on the relative merits of each director's objectives and the priorities of the overall organization.

In this revised approach, the chancellor has given each of his directors an opportunity to compete for the available resources. In effect he has said, "Tell me what you should be doing during 1974, justify it, and then we'll determine how much of the resources you will be awarded." Now, he's practicing a motivational approach to planning.

THE UPDATED VERSION IN PRACTICE

The rightful position of budgets can be seen by viewing the format of a typical profit plan for an organization operating under MBO. Figure 1 is a simplified version of the profit plan constructed under a motivational approach. The budget flows from objectives, not vice versa.

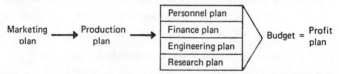

Fig. 1. Position of the budget in a profit plan prepared under the "motivational" approach. The manager in charge of each of the six major functions prepares his operating plan, containing his objectives and plans to achieve them. The operating plans are coordinated with all managers on a need-to-know basis. Then a budget is prepared. The budget thus flows from the objectives and plans.

This format clearly indicates the budget in its proper position. This positioning promotes what is commonly referred to as the motivational approach to profit planning. The manager begins his planning with practically unlimited opportunity to optimize his results. He knows that his results are limited only by his ability to justify the contribution he can make. He doesn't begin his planning with a budgetary constraint. Figure 2 illustrates the position of the budget in a "fiscal" approach to planning. The objectives flow from the budget.

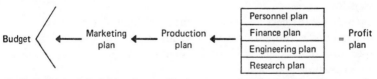

Fig. 2 Position of the budget in a profit plan prepared under the "fiscal" approach. The budget is enunciated first and then objectives and plans are written to support the budget. Objectives and plans thus flow from the budget. This is an outgrowth of the "fiscal" approach to planning, i.e., revenue was projected, then costs were projected, and the difference constituted the objective.

THE PLANNING SEQUENCE

The relationship of budgeting to planning and the role budgets should play can be illustrated by following the step-by-step sequence of the preparation of a profit plan for a particular year. The calendar year 1974 will be used in this illustration:

Step 1

The top management of the organization issues what is commonly referred to as "the call for the profit plan" for 1974. Typically, this call is issued by the chief executive officer to each of the officers reporting to him.

This call will contain the following information to be used as guidance for lower levels of management as they prepare their "operating plans" (objectives and plans to achieve them):

a. The overall objectives of the organization for 1974.

b. An analysis of the outside environment as it may impact on the company's operations in 1974, e.g., the competitive picture, the economy in general, the industry picture, etc.

c. The priorities of the company during 1974.

d. The major assumptions on which the 1974 overall corporate objectives have been based.

e. The ground rules to be followed by lower level managers when preparing their operating plans.

f. A timetable for preparing the operating plans.

The manager should already be in possession of an approved long-range plan—commonly covering five years—for his department. This, of course, provides him with considerable guidance as he prepares his 1974 plans and objectives.

Step 2

Each of the officers and department heads completes the necessary analysis and coordination with other managers and then submits his operating plan covering all of his operations for 1974. In essence, his operating plan will include:

a. The objectives recommended for the target period.

b. The plans by which each of the objectives will be achieved. (Sometimes referred to as "programming the objectives.")

c. "Ball Park" numbers as to what the objectives and plans mean in terms of revenues, expenses, and rates of return, plus capital required.

In effect, each of these managers is preparing an estimated budget covering his planned operations. It is emphasized that the manager prepares this budget *after* determining what he plans to accomplish. He does not begin his planning with a set of budget figures handed to him from above.

Step 3
This step comprises the analysis and consolidation of the operating plans of all of the officers into a total profit plan for the organization (see Fig. 1).

a. The operating plans of all of the officers and their departments will be subjected to a penetrating financial analysis and a consolidated budget will be prepared for the total company.

b. The president and his staff* will review the total profit plan for consistency with company objectives, ground rules, and priorities.

c. The president may discuss with each of his officers the officer's operating plan and suggest revisions or complete changes.

d. A consolidated budget is prepared reflecting the changes resulting from *c,* above. Resources are allocated to the objectives based upon how well each manager competed for the available resources and the priorities which have been set for the target period.

e. The consolidated budget is compared to the overall objectives of the corporation for the target period.

f. If the consolidated budget is consistent with the corporate objectives, the operating plans are approved.

g. If the consolidated budget is not consistent with the corporate objectives, one of two approaches will be followed:

    (1) The operating plans will be returned to the officers for ad-

---

*The president's staff in this case may include the financial officer, the top planning manager, and other staff specialists. In some cases it may include a budget committee.

ditional analysis and efforts to try to bring them up to the corporate objectives, or,

(2) The operating plans—if considered valid—are accepted and the corporate objectives are adjusted accordingly.

Additional comment is in order with respect to *g*, above. The hallmarks of an achievement-oriented manager are twofold; (1) a willingness to take the necessary time and effort to arrive at well-formulated objectives and plans in the first place and, (2) a complete unwillingness to adjust the objectives downward unless there is absolutely no alternative action which he can take to prevent the downward adjustment.

Thus, in *g* above, when all of the individual operating plans do not add up to the overall corporate objectives, the first recourse should not be to lower the overall objectives. First, complete emphasis should be devoted to leaving the objectives at their present levels and then pursuing all possible alternatives for overcoming the void.

Step 4

Figure 1 indicates that preparation of the budget is the concluding part of the profit plan. And this is an accurate portrayal when the profit plan is viewed for a particular target period, say one year.

However, in a very real sense, there is never a "conclusion" to the planning process—it is a continuous and ongoing part of the job of all managers. Once the profit plan has been approved, it is not filed away to be removed from the files and read some time in the future. It must be looked upon as a viable, living document which the manager uses as the major guide for his day-to-day actions. Actual performance against the plan will be evaluated as the year unfolds. Certain revisions will be necessary during the year to keep the plan realistic. The experience gained with the plan during one year will serve as the basis for much of what is included in the profit plans for subsequent years.

Thus, the planning process should be considered as a continuous circle or loop in which:

a. Objectives, plans, and budgets are prepared for a particular target period.

b. The objectives, plans, and budgets are approved and the manager begins operating under his plan.

c. Results versus plan are evaluated continuously during the target period and at the conclusion of it.

d. The entire process is repeated beginning with the preparation of objectives, plans, and budgets for the next target period.

CONCLUSION

Budgets have a key role to play in the MBO system but they are not an end in themselves. Once properly viewed and constructed, they provide a valuable vehicle for controlling or monitoring; however; their primary thrust should not be for control purposes.

The primary thrust of budgeting must be to motivate managers to optimize their results. Control is a secondary, later consideration and should come about as a by-product—not as the main product.

The transition from "control" to "motivational" budgeting necessitates a change not only in the positioning of the budget but, also, a rather radical change in the position and orientation of the budget director. Traditionally, he has been a member of the controller's staff and as such has had a financial statement orientation of looking backwards at what has already happened. He must start considering himself as a member of the management team looking ahead. A backward orientation implies control. A forward orientation permits the motivational approach.

This transition is not easily made. It requires a radical departure from decades of training and practice which emphasized the function of the budget director as one who looked at corporate life through a rearview mirror where he often saw little but controls, reports, and variances. Unfortunately, even today, only a few schools of business approach budgeting from an MBO, motivational approach.

The motivational approach to budgeting requires that:

a. Competition for resources be emphasized.

b. Results not be predetermined by beginning the planning process with budgetary allocations.

c. Each manager be permitted and encouraged to demonstrate the contribution which he is capable of making, before resources are awarded.

d. Budgets should flow from objectives. Objectives should not flow from budgets.

Management by Objectives, properly implemented and directed, is a potent means for motivating managers to greater performance. MBO is an achievement-oriented approach. The role of budgets must be one which capitalizes on the motivational qualities which are inherent in the system.

PROGRESS AND PERFORMANCE REVIEW—
FEEDBACK FOR MANAGING ACCOUNTABILITY

Review and evaluation complete the MBO/R cycle. They must be handled periodically throughout the year and not just at a set time the way traditional performance reviews, often called performance appraisals, are characteristically done. Monthly, or quarterly, progress reviews are a way to provide the opportunity for a regular review and evaluation of RESULTS and the performance review will provide the interface with the total system on an annual basis.

Feedback systems provide much of the basic data necessary for these review and evaluation sessions. In addition, the parties in the review will share their own feedback with each other. This will include subjective evaluations based on criteria agreed upon at the beginning of the evaluation period.

FEEDBACK SYSTEMS

After the desired RESULTS have been determined, it is necessary to identify the feedback system that will tell individuals and groups when the RESULTS are achieved. An effective feedback system is one in which the person or group doing the job receives information in a form and at a time that allows it to be used to evaluate performance against standards and to take corrective action if necessary. The primary sources of information are accounting reports, sales records, records checks, sight check (visual inspection), internal surveys, external surveys, and secondary data.[1]

When a standard is developed, the feedback systems need to be identified or developed at the same time. Care must be exercised that duplicate systems are not created as the information needed may already be in existence in the management information system. It is appropriate to evaluate periodically management information systems for their effectiveness. Those responsible for information systems should be accountable for information utilization and/or information availability (RESULTS) rather than compilation and reporting (activities).

The *first* condition of an effective feedback system is that the data goes to the person or group in a position to make corrections if the operation is below standard. Unfortunately, under traditional management systems the feedback usually goes to upper levels of management who tell lower levels what to do when a correction is necessary. In this case the subordinate receives his feedback through his boss, who also provides him with the solution to the problem. Consequently the subordinate is likely to be accountable only for activities, not for RESULTS. Under this approach when there is a malfunction the subordinate asks the boss for the solution or decision. He is not expected to make any decisions on his own, even though he may have the capability and resources to do so.

Under RESULTS-oriented management, the form of the feedback should vary by different levels in the organization. The amount that any one manager receives will be based on what is needed for self-evaluation of the performance expected of him. Consequently, upper levels of management should not receive feedback in the detail that operators and lower levels of management would. The operator needs the information in sufficient detail to make the corrections in the operation. The manager needs the information necessary to *manage* the operation and evaluate performance. In other words, it is appropriate that there be a hierarchy of reports.

The *second* condition of an effective feedback system is that it is timely. An individual needs the feedback in a time frame that permits corrective action. For instance, a budget performance report two months late is of little help, whereas ten days after the end of the month it is helpful.

Some feedback systems are automatic and immediate, such as the assembly of a radio that is plugged in and tested. A salesman quite often receives immediate feedback on his efforts. It may be appropriate that an individual or group keep some of its own data to ensure its timeliness.

The *third* condition is that the data is supplied in a form that the individual using it can readily find and understand. Existing systems need to be evaluated on whether the information supplied is appropriate, or if the appropriate information is supplied. The question "Why?" should be asked on all information supplied in order to eliminate nonessential data.

A *fourth* condition for an effective feedback system is that it meet an acceptable standard of quality and accuracy. If the user does not trust the data, he will not use them and may develop a duplicate system of his own.

A *fifth* condition is that the feedback system meet the cost-and-benefit test. A checking of the feedback system from this standpoint may result in a reduced, less costly system that meets other conditions of an effective system. For example, it may be found that a sampling approach or a periodic check may be adequate and it is not necessary to do the complete tabulation continuously.

The best way to maintain an effective feedback system is to hold those responsible for the reporting systems accountable for their usage and availability. This results in joint accountability for both the issuer and the user of the information.

PROGRESS REVIEWS

It is necessary to answer these questions about progress reviews: "What is the purpose of progress reviews?" "What decisions are going to be made as a result of these reviews?" Focusing on the answers to these questions will help prevent progress reviews from becoming another activity that is being performed because it is one of the steps in the MBO/R system.

The purpose of progress reviews is largely developmental. To achieve this purpose, both objectives and standards will be evaluated and corrective action and improvement will be discussed. A dialogue on what real performance is may take place. Performance needs always to be checked against the MBO/R navigation system. Dialogue provides an opportunity for the boss to coach and counsel employees and for the boss to develop mutual trust with employees. Out of these reviews may come new or revised objectives on both the task and the development of the individual employee. The objectives for the employee may be for the development of needed skills and knowledge.

It is essential that progress reviews be held on both an individual and organization basis: boss-subordinate, boss-team, and/or the group working on an organization objective. The boss has the responsibility to see that this occurs.

It has been our experience that many MBO systems stop with the boss-subordinate goal setting. It is just as important, perhaps *more* important, for the team to hold progress reviews also. This also applies to a group from different functions working on an organization objective. This is where the individual interfaces with the organization and the progress on the horizontal relationships, the interdependency, can be reviewed. The team progress reviews will be supportive of the boss-subordinate progress reviews relative to an employee's effectiveness in his ability to work with his peers. The team sessions will enable both the boss and subordinate to evaluate progress on this item. As in the boss-subordinate progress review, the team will look at its objectives, recognize achievement, analyze variances from the action plan and standards, and develop plans for correction. Role relationships will be looked at regularly and new role contracts may be negotiated. This is also where the team will manage accountability by confronting nonperformance and broken contracts.

Progress reviews should be held monthly, but this may vary according to the individual's responsibility, the trust level, the availability of boss and subordinate, and the complexity of the work. In reality the progress review may be a part of a checkpoint meeting in the action plan of an objective, or may be a separate session. Its length may vary from an hour or less to half a day or a whole day, depending on what has to be discussed. The interval between reviews will probably be shorter in the early stages of MBO/R implementation to develop the skills in working this way, to demonstrate the commitment to the MBO/R process, and to fully clarify expectations (psychological contracting) the boss and subordinate have of each other. We worked with a typical manager who started with weekly reviews and gradually switched to monthly reviews.

The boss needs to be, aware that the time interval between progress reviews and the way of handling these reviews may vary from one employee to another depending on the employee's value system as discussed in Chapter 2.

(1) Tribalistic values will favor more group reviews with directive leadership. (2) Egocentric values will dictate frequent reviews, one-to-one, with considerable direction and demands. (3) Conformity values will prefer more structured reviews, more one-to-one, and much direction. (4) Manipulative values will want more indirect leadership, emphasis on achievement, and probably more one-to-one and fewer group meetings. (5) Sociocentric values will emphasize more group evaluation and shared leadership. It probably will be necessary to emphasize accountability with people having these values. (6) Existential values will prefer a nondirective style of leadership and few meetings.

At this progress review step there is the potential for conflict over accountability and differences. Being aware of this, the boss and the group should develop their skills to deal with conflict in a constructive way that will provide a positive influence on the setting and achievement of future objectives. This is an application of Talbot's management of differences.[2]

PERFORMANCE REVIEWS

The purpose of the performance review is evaluating the interface of the individual with the system. In it there is an evaluation of the performance of the individual in meeting the expectations of the system agreed upon at the beginning of the evaluation period.[3] It should produce data for manpower planning, career planning, and salary determination. The interface of the performance review (appraisal) subsystem with the human resource system is discussed in *A Systems Look at Performance Appraisal* by Slusher at the end of this chapter. While evaluation takes place in both reviews, the performance review is a more formal part of the process than the progress review which is largely problem solving. The performance review will produce some documents that will go into the personal file of the employee.[4] The progress reviews will produce data that can be used in the performance review, but will also help the climate in the performance reviews because the interface between the boss and subordinate has been occurring regularly and is not just a once-a-year occasion.

The performance review is essentially a boss-subordinate review, but as an organization has more experience with MBO/R and there is a more open climate, a team performance review is recommended. This review is usually held annually, but some organizations require it more often.

In the past, MBO has been installed in some organizations to shore up a sagging performance appraisal system. The purpose in these situations appears to be largely evaluative and control, making it difficult for effective use of the MBO/R concept. This is discussed in the Wikstrom article.[4]

REWARDS

The handling of rewards determines the credibility of MBO/R. The distribution of rewards on a basis other than performance and RESULTS could destroy the MBO/R concept in the eyes of employees. Salary and monetary rewards are probably the most tangible rewards. Consequently organizations embarking on the MBO/R concept should review the salary and monetary rewards systems early in the implementation process and start action on revision if the present system is not supportive. The performance data coming out of progress reviews and feedback systems should greatly increase the objectivity of management's decisions on the distribution of rewards, but a degree of subjectivity will still remain with the manager. One of the difficult aspects of this approach is the willingness and ability of a manager to confront the nonperformer face-to-face and tell him why he is not receiving rewards. The individual manager needs to have a high degree of control over salary and monetary-rewards decisions for his subordinates. This is managing accountability.

In some systems, e.g., government civil service, a manager has little control over salary decisions. However, he usually has more control than he is willing to take and use. A manager in some of these systems often remarks, "I cannot fire a nonperformer." Experience shows that a nonperformer can be fired, but it may be a messy, difficult procedure and the manager is unwilling to take the risk or expend the energy necessary. One manager in government remarked that he had fired numerous nonperformers and it had been difficult and also that he had been reversed in several cases. His stand was that he had to go to this trouble and take this risk if he expected performance from his staff.

It must also be remembered that there are usually many other recognized rewards other than money. These include special projects and assignments, special training and education, attendance at conferences and conventions, representing the boss, etc. These will vary in different organizations.

The question of handling salary review at the same time as the performance review is controversial. Ultimately, they should be handled together. However in the first few years of an MBO/R implementation it may be advisable to separate the two, holding the salary review several months before or after the performance review. It is necessary that the employee feel free to evaluate his performance in the performance review without the threat that if he admits deficiencies and mistakes, it will affect his salary increase. In other words, self-protection may get in the path of self-evaluation.

COMPLETED CYCLE

Progress and performance reviews are the last steps in the MBO/R operation system. In reality after the MBO/R concept is fully operational the steps will tend to flow together and the lines of demarcation between each step will not be readily distinguishable. For example, a checkpoint meeting in an action plan may also include the progress review, planning analysis, and objective setting steps. The value of the MBO/R model here is to verify that all operational steps are being carried out and to regularly check that the steps are supportive of and within the boundaries of the mission, roles and effectiveness areas as established in the navigation system. Thus we are making MBO/R work by *managing* for organization RE-SULTS.

NOTES

1. W.J. Reddin 1972. *Effective management by objectives.* New York: McGraw-Hill, pp. 101-105.

2. See *The Development of Power Relationships in Management* by John C. Talbot in Chapter 3.

3. Hughes and Flowers list five items as being necessary for job per-formance—knowledge, skills, health, availability, and attitude. This is an innovative approach to the human resources accounting concept and may be helpful in structuring a performance review.
   V.S. Flowers and B.A. Coda 1974. Human resource planning: foundation for a model. *Personnel* (January-February). pp. 20-42.

4. We do not intend to go into depth in this chapter as much has been written in support of our position on performance review. Chapter 8 of Beck and Hillmar's *A practical approach to organization development through MBO* contains a good summary of the subject and two out-standing articles, Goal-oriented approaches to people and job measurement, by Charles Hughes and Management by objectives or appraisal by results, by Walter Wikstrom.

A SYSTEMS LOOK AT PERFORMANCE APPRAISAL

E. ALLEN SLUSHER

One of the most successful contemporary approaches to analyzing management problems is systems theory. The systems viewpoint encourages us to take a broader and more analytical approach to familiar problems. One such familiar problem, for which systems theory provides an enlarged perspective, is performance appraisal.

Reprinted by permission of the publisher from the *Personnel Journal* (February) 1975. © 1975 *Personnel Journal.*

Few issues have been as widely discussed and written about. Unfortunately, these dialogues and articles have tended to focus on discrete aspects of appraisal, while ignoring the interconnection between aspects. Typical articles deal with rating scales, appraisal interviews or appraisor position (i.e., superior, subordinate or peer). While each of these topics is important and merits extended discussion, this piecemeal approach has led to confusion about the full potential of performance appraisal. Some experts have even questioned the propriety of traditional appraisal methods. Despite this confusion and doubt, most organizations continue to conduct formal appraisals, although the sophistication of such programs varies widely. Even in those instances where no formal appraisal is made, informal judgments about individual performance are inescapable.

THE HUMAN RESOURCE SYSTEM

The pervasiveness of performance appraisal results from the crucial role it plays in managing the organization's human resources. This role can be clearly seen when performance appraisal is examined in a systems context. The flowchart shown in Exhibit 1 depicts a typical human resource system.

This system manifests several characteristics common to all systems. First, the human resource system is differentiated from other organizational systems by a *boundary* (indicated by the dotted line in Exhibit 1). What should be included within the boundary (i.e., what comprises the system) depends on the analyst's intent in conceptualizing the system. Thus, it is clearly useful for our purposes here to distinguish between a human resource system and a technological system or a financial system, although it should be realized that these three systems do affect each other. For another purpose it might be useful to consider the three systems as combined into a larger system. The existence of a system boundary implies that those elements not within the system lie in a larger *suprasystem* or environment. The suprasystem affects the system by providing *inputs* to the system and accepting *outputs* from the system.

In the human resource system presented here, there are three inputs: organizational goals, human talent and other suprasystem factors. By providing the residual input ("other environmental

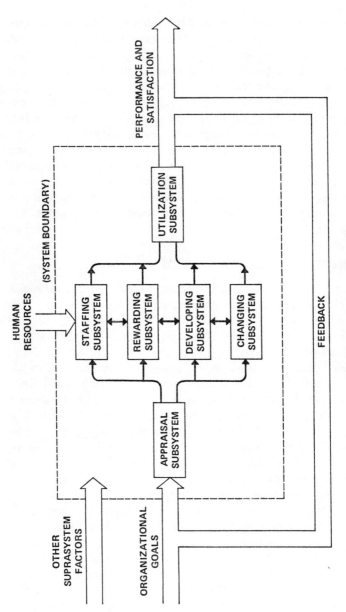

Exhibit 1 Human resource system.

factors"), we are clearly de-emphasizing the individual significance of these factors for our current analysis. However, this input is included as a reminder that we may later wish to increase the complexity and generality of our analysis by considering these suprasystem inputs in more detail. The outputs from the human resource system are organizational performance and human need satisfaction. By meeting performance standards, the organization strives to ensure its own survival. Persons participate in the organization and society sanctions its existence because the organization supplies at least a minimal level of need satisfaction to its internal participants and external clients. When a system is characterized by inputs and outputs, it is termed an *open system*. The openness of a system permits it to grow and adapt to a changing environment. In contrast, the *closed system* does not interact with its suprasystem through inputs and outputs. The closed system eventually decays and dies. Although a system may be viewed as closed in the short run, in the long run all systems are open. Thus, we are really describing degrees of openness or closedness at some point in time.

The openness or closedness of a system can be a useful concept to the human resource manager. Each manager is faced with numerous day-to-day activities and problems. In meeting these daily demands, the manager quite appropriately treats the system as closed and seeks to fine tune its internal functioning. His specialized expertise and assigned responsibilities conspire to reinforce this closed system view. However, when a manager exclusively acts as if a system is closed when it is in fact open, he loses perspective on the system's role. Since the manager has great influence in the system, treating an open system as if it were closed, he in effect reduces actual openness. That is, managers can directly influence the openness or closedness of an organizational system by their decisions and viewpoint. For example, the manager with a relatively closed system view will be less likely to nurture beneficial contacts with pertinent organizational areas. Because the link between a system and the larger organizational suprasystem is through inputs and outputs, treating a system as closed leads to divergence between organizational goals and system activity. We too frequently observe such excessive instances of closed system thinking as "empire building" and managing "blinders." In contrast, the open system perspective emphasizes that systems meet objectives by ingesting appropriate inputs. As effective managers, we must not forget that the human resource system should be directed toward organizational goals. This admonition will be easier to follow when we adopt an open system perspective.

Another useful systems concept is *holism*. Systems are more than the sum of their individual parts. The holistic concept stresses the need to analyze a system as a unified whole by focusing on the interaction between systems parts. This system view sharply contrasts with the typical manager's propensity to "get things straight" in one department, program or activity before considering the next problem. The human resource system contains several subsystems or elements. Six such subsystems are identified in the system flowchart shown in Exhibit 1. These subsystems interact with one another as indicated by the arrows. Within the utilization-subsystem's jobs, programs and assignments, the organization's work is accomplished. There are four subsystems which directly support this utilization subsystem. The "staffing" subsystem brings human resources into the organization and places them in appropriate positions in the utilization subsystem. People work because they receive various desired outcomes from the "rewarding" subsystem. The human resource potential is enhanced through a "developing" subsystem, and necessary modifications of the organization are made through a "changing" subsystem. The staffing, rewarding, developing, and changing subsystems that support the utilization subsystem are interrelated as highlighted by the two-way arrows through the center of the flowchart. However, for our purposes here, the most salient interactions occur between the appraisal subsystem and the four supporting subsystems.

APPRAISAL AS A FEEDBACK MECHANISM

As the flowchart dramatizes, the appraisal subsystem serves as the *feedback* mechanism for the human resource system. It is the feedback aspect which gives the open system its goal-directed quality. Since the resource system should be guided by the organization's goals, it is mandatory to determine how performance compares to objectives. When performance is inferior, feedback alerts the system to needed improvement; if performance is above current objectives, then more challenging objectives may be appropriate.

As the feedback mechanism, the appraisal subsystem plays a crucial role in managing the human resource system.

Feedback through appraisal can be comprehended more fully by investigating the potential *interfaces* or contacts between the appraisal subsystem and the support subsystems. Some of these potential interfaces are summarized in Exhibit 2.

When examining these interfaces, it is essential to notice that the appraisal subsystem is broader in scope than the traditional performance review session, at fixed intervals, between a superior and a subordinate. Although formal review sessions are a major element in the appraisal subsystem, there are numerous other potential elements which must be carefully designed to meet interface requirements. Appraisal is multifaceted and far too crucial to rely only on formal reviews requiring a few hours each year. When examining Exhibit 2, it will be instructive to consider three questions: (1) What are your organization's current appraisal interfaces? (2) What should your appraisal interfaces be? and (3) How effective are your interfaces? It is indeed a rare organization which exploits all potential appraisal interfaces and executes each effectively.

As Exhibit 2 illustrates, appraisals should be conceptualized as primarily developmental for the individual and/or the organization. Only three of the sixteen appraisal interfaces are categorized as judgmental or evaluative in intent. Judgmental decisions must be made about promotions, terminations, and merit increases. These decisions require an historical review to determine who is at fault and who should be congratulated. However, the major focus of appraisal should be future-oriented. Improving future organizational performance and enhancing employee potential should be the primary concern when managing the human resource system.

Exhibit 2 shows that each support subsystem contains certain major elements. The appraisal subsystem may not interface with all of these elements in a significant way. For example, the benefits and salary structure elements in an organization's rewarding subsystem are influenced most directly by general economic conditions and the

Subsystems Elements	Interface with Appraisal Subsystem	Viewpoint
Staffing:		
Recruitment	Identifying current inadequacies	Developmental
Selection	Criteria for selection predictors	Developmental
Placement	—	—
Transfer	Individual skills for new assignment	Developmental
Promotion	Identifying outstanding performer	Judgmental
Termination	Identifying inadequate performer	Judgmental
Human resource inventory	Skill and potential data	Developmental
Rewarding:		
Benefits	—	—
Salary structure	—	—
Merit	Comparative data on performance	Judgmental
Intrinsic	Motivation through objective setting, feedback and participation	Developmental
Changing:		
Organizational climate	Appraisee evaluation	Developmental
Organizational structure	—	—
Management styles	Identify need for general change	Developmental
Policies	Two-way feedback	Developmental
Communication	Two-way feedback	Developmental
Developing:		
Rotating	Judgments on learning	Developmental
Training	Identifying individual upgrading needs	Developmental
	Evaluating previous training	Developmental
Counseling	Career planning basis	Developmental

Exhibit 2 Appraisal Interfaces

local competition for human resources. Thus, it is efficient to first examine those interfaces where appraisal has a direct and significant impact.

The employee's initial contact with the organization occurs in the staffing subsystem's recruitment element. Complex, integrated modern organizations no longer permit the luxury of seeking merely "bodies." Appraisal methods must be used to assess which skills and professional talents are required. When prospective employees have been identified, selection procedures should be based on criteria developed by comparing the appraised behavioral differences between effective and ineffective current and past employees. After an employee is placed in a job, transfers should be based on appraisal of present and potential skills applicable to the new assignment. Appraisals are the basis for constructing human resource inventories which are immediately useful in recruiting, planning and developing activities. Such an inventory is a prerequisite for human resource accounting.

The rewarding subsystem's major developmental activity is providing intrinsic rewards which increase employee motivation. The appraisal subsystem can be used to give employees an opportunity to help set individual objectives, to receive feedback on performance, and to participate more fully in shaping their careers. These factors will serve to enhance employee motivation. Programs like Management by Objectives directly attempt to provide each performance feedback and participatory goal setting.

Appraisal need not be exclusively a process where the organization evaluates the employee. It is also helpful to have employees appraise the organization and to use these appraisals as inputs to decisions regarding organizational change. Thus, employee evaluations of organization's psychological climate, policies and formal communications should be starting points for anticipated change programs. In the same sense, general programs to change management styles are inappropriate until sound evidence concerning current styles is available.

The most prominent developmental implications of appraisal involve interfaces with the developing subsystem. Far too many organizations continue to train employees with general programs unsuited to individual needs. Appraisal should be used to spot those areas where an employee requires specific skill development that is directly related to current and future job performance. With this approach, maximal use of scarce training dollars can be assured. Moreover, appraisals can help determine the success of past training. Regrettably often, concern for training ends with the formal session. Appraisals should also constitute the basis for career counseling between an employee and his supervisor or appropriate personnel specialists. When career guidance is based on performance and not on personality, its impact will be greater. Finally, job rotation should depend on appraised learning and not a formal, fixed time schedule.

The systems viewpoint enables us to develop a broader perspective on the management of human resources. Too often, specialists and functional managers of human resources see their responsibility areas as closed subsystems. They fail to discern interactions between their subsystem and other subsystems. Thus, they begin to lose sight of the human resource system as a whole and its mission to contribute to organizational goal attainment.

Examining the organization's human resources as a system emphasizes that managing human resources is not exclusively a personnel function. Personnel does play a central role, especially in the recruitment and selection elements of the staffing subsystem, in the benefits and salary structure elements of the rewarding subsystem and in the training of the developing subsystem. However, managers throughout the organization have integral roles in the other subsystem elements. Human resources constitute the one pervasive aspect of every organization and the complex organization's most valuable asset.

The human resource system's ability as an open system, to progress toward organizational goals, depends chiefly on the supply of comprehensive feedback from the appraisal subsystem. The appraisal subsystem's feedback contribution can be fully understood by analyzing resource subsystems. Few organizations utilize all the potential feedback interfaces that sound appraisal offers. Moreover, appraisal's full potential can be realized only when it is conceptualized as a multifaceted process rather than simply an annual review session. Most managers can profit from a hard systems look at their appraisal subsystem. It is through careful, continuous appraisal that the organization's human resources are directed toward the organization's goals.

SUGGESTED READINGS

Beatty, Richard W., 1973. "Personnel systems and human performance." *Personnel Journal*, 53, 307–312.

Cummings, L.L., and D.W. Schwab, 1973. *Performance in Organizations: Determinants and Appraisal.* Scott Foresman.

Rieder, George A., 1972. "Performance review—a mixed bag." *Personnel Administrator*, 17, November-December, 25–27.

Schuster, Fred, 1971. "A systems approach to managing human resources." *Personnel Administrator*, 16, March-April, 27–32.

DEVELOPING THE MBO/R SKILLS AND COMPETENCIES TO MAKE IT HAPPEN

The adoption of the MBO/R concept will undoubtedly require new skills and competencies in an organization. This is a basic reason for moving slowly, but deliberately, in implementing this concept so that these new skills and competencies can be learned through experience and development.

The development of skills and competencies for effective MBO/R can be broken down into four parts: (1) diagnosis of needs; (2) using MBO/R to facilitate the change; (3) consulting and training relationships; and (4) supportive subjects.

DIAGNOSIS OF NEEDS

This diagnostic process is an ongoing one. Certain needed skills and competencies for both individuals and units will be identified in the beginning and others will become evident as the organization moves through the implementation process. We prefer to develop these skills and competencies as the need is identified rather than embarking on a wholesale development program based on the assumption that everyone will need certain skills eventually. The training program for implementing MBO/R should be designed to be responsive to individuals and groups making MBO/R work. The trainers are jointly accountable with managers for successful implementation.

To help in diagnosing the needed skills and competencies three models are recommended.

1. The systemic model described in Chapter 6 enables the organization to take a global look at the total process including MBO/R, Organization Development, human systems and human resources.

2. The Membership—Control—Production model in Chapter 3 enables management to look at the emPOWERment issue in more detail as it relates to membership and production including such behavioral items as differences, norms, roles, and structure.

3. The MBO/R navigation and operation model enables the organization to see the total MBO/R process and determine where they are in the process and in what steps they may need help.

The use of these three theory models can be helpful in both identifying where there are skill and competency deficiencies and understanding why and how they are important in the total process.

USING MBO/R TO FACILITATE CHANGE

The first question to ask when management is considering the MBO/R concept is "Why MBO/R?" What is it that management wishes to change? What performance or output is it after? What conditions will exist when the desired RESULTS are achieved? Unless these questions are answered, there is a danger that MBO/R might be the right answer to the wrong problem.

By using the MBO/R concept in putting MBO/R into practice, the emphasis on *managing* and RESULTS will be maintained. The MBO/R navigation and operation model could be used for this purpose. The outcome desired in such effectiveness areas as subordinates, co-workers, innovation, systems, and development will be identified. This will provide the basis for accountability in the area of management, as well as the task.

This *managing* for RESULTS approach to MBO/R implementation will facilitate management's evaluation of the concept and determination of its appropriateness for the organization. A possible outcome may be that the organization is not ready for MBO/R and other alternatives should be explored.

CONSULTING AND TRAINING RELATIONSHIPS

An ongoing consulting and training support system is necessary in implementing MBO/R. However, these functions can be performed in a number of different ways by different people, including external consultants, internal consultants and trainers, and by individual managers. Each organization must determine its own approach to this after identifying the needs and the existing resources within its organization.

External consultants can be utilized through (1) public seminars, (2) training sessions within the organization, (3) consulting with individuals and groups within the organization, and (4) books and publication articles.

Public seminars are helpful in the early stages to achieve an understanding of the MBO/R concept for making a decision on whether to use it. They may also be used to evaluate the approaches of several consultants to determine the best approach for a particular organization, and whether an external consultant could work effectively with the organization.

Public seminars can also be used to train new management personnel and to obtain help on problems that managers are experiencing in using the MBO/R concept. One manager used public seminars by attending, with other members of the top management team, several seminars conducted by different consultants. With these approaches they developed their own system and performed the training and consulting function themselves. An external consultant was retained periodically to help with special problems and to evaluate progress. This particular organization had a high degree of success with this approach.

External consultants can also be used effectively to conduct training sessions within the organization, to consult with individual managers and groups on special problems, and to develop internal consultants, facilitators, or advisers. The organization may use one external consultant on a continuing basis or different consultants to meet specialized needs. In any event the use of external consultants should decrease as the implementation process proceeds and the organization is able to handle this function internally. Care should be exercised that management does not become dependent on an external consultant.

Books and articles by consultants should be used extensively and be constantly available. An ongoing literature search needs to be maintained for the latest research and findings.[1]

Internal consultants, sometimes called facilitators, trainers, or MBO advisers, are desirable because their help needs to be available when an individual manager or group wants it. Their role is best described as follows: "The adviser is present at all sessions throughout the implementation. The purpose of the adviser's presence is fourfold: (1) to ensure that process requirements are met; (2) to instruct where necessary; (3) to ensure adequate communications and understanding between participants; and (4) to evaluate effectiveness of the MBO process application, assess problems with implementation, and propose and assist with corrective actions."[2] This is more of an on-the-job training approach after workshop participation.

In England and Canada, MBO advisers are being used extensively. It is important that these advisers have high competence and credibility. They may have been trainers or managers. In one department in Canadian government more than 20 MBO advisers were selected to help implement MBO in a 12,000 employee department. Many of those chosen for this role were successful managers who were given this full-time assignment for two or three years. It must be emphasized that advisers or internal consultants should be in a collaborative role—joint responsibility—with managers and do not have the sole responsibility for MBO implementation, as MBO *cannot* be delegated. Effective use of the MBO concept is the joint responsibility of the manager and the consultant.

Individual managers may operate as trainers and consultants with their units. This is a good approach as the manager will more likely internalize it. However, the drawback may be that the manager's behavior may be a barrier and subordinates may be unwilling to be open and take risks with him. A third-party consultant can help this relationship. A combination of the managerial effort plus the third-party consultant probably is a better approach.

SUPPORTIVE SUBJECTS

In addition to basic training on MBO/R technical skills such as objective writing, training on other needed skills and competencies will fall into four major categories: (1) group process skills; (2) interpersonal skills; (3) systems; and (4) awareness of self. All of these, of course, are in addition to the basic technical skills and knowledge needed for a particular job. Some of the items in these four categories are as follows:

1) Group process skills
   (a) Team building
   (b) Goal setting
   (c) Problem solving and decision making
   (d) Process consultation

2) Interpersonal skills
   (a) Managing differences/conflict
   (b) Diagnosis and feedback
   (c) Managing accountability
   (d) Managing the helping relationship
   (e) Interviewing
   (f) Counseling and coaching

3) Systems
   (a) Systems development
   (b) Management information systems
   (c) Job design/job enrichment
   (d) Work simplification
   (e) Organization/physical structure
   (f) Planning
   (g) Salary and rewards systems
   (h) Open systems
   (i) PERT, Gantt, Critical Path Systems

4) Awareness of self
   (a) Transactional Analysis
   (b) Gestalt techniques
   (c) Reality Therapy
   (d) Values clarification
   (e) Sensitivity training
   (f) Personal growth

Obviously all of these will not be used in any one organization. This checklist can be valuable in diagnosing needs and determining the priorities for training and development for individuals and units. Supportive training needs to cover three areas: (1) knowledge (theory), (2) skills (applying theory successfully), and (3) awareness of self. The third area of awareness is often neglected and may unknowingly be a barrier to the use of knowledge and skills. Considerable progress is being made on developing awareness in managers through the application of Gestalt techniques, Transactional Analysis, and values clarification to organization problems.

SUMMARY

In concluding this book we summarize that there is complexity to implementing the MBO/R concept. It will require a high commitment on the part of management to provide the necessary resources and time for successful implementation. As mentioned earlier, we recommend slow deliberate working of the process with the commitment to "hang in there" when the going gets tough. MBO/R is a sound concept that can be helpful in managing change in a downturn as well as in prosperous times. We emphasize again the need to focus on *managing* for RESULTS!

NOTES

1. The monthly *Management by Objectives Newsletter* written by George S. Odiorne is very helpful on MBO literature search.
2. Frank R. Hinton. *Management by objectives—concepts and process.* Bureau of Management Consulting, Government of Canada.